WORLD WAR

IN

MORAY

1939 - 1945

BILL BARTLAM
and
IAN KEILLAR

Librario

Published by

Librario Publishing Ltd.

ISBN No: 1-904440-36-3

Copies can be ordered from retail
or via the internet at:
www.librario.com

or from:

Brough House
Milton Brodie
Kinloss
Moray
IV36 2UA
Tel / Fax: 01343 850617

Printed in Times (11pt)

Layout by Steven James
www.chimeracreations.co.uk

Printed and bound by
Antony Rowe Ltd., Eastbourne

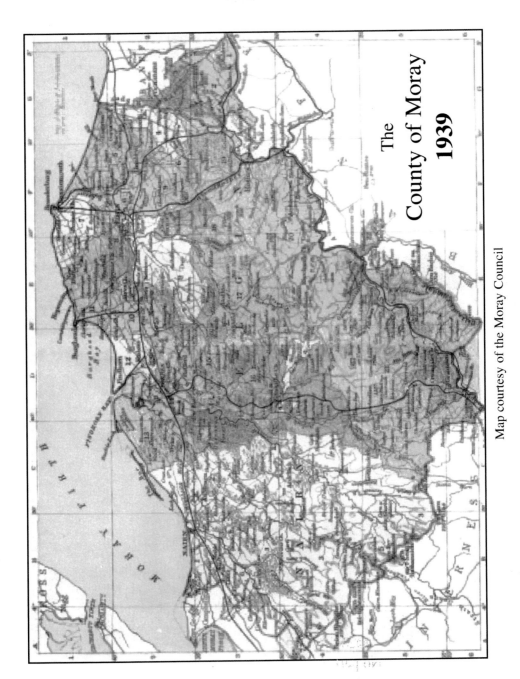

The
County of Moray
1939

Map courtesy of the Moray Council

Unit signs seen in Moray during World War II

3 INF DIV

79 ARMD DIV

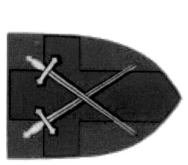

SECOND ARMY

21 ARMY GROUP

The Authors are indebted to The Moray Council

for financial assistance in publishing this work.

This work is dedicated to the Men and Women of Moray who went off to war in 1939-45 and who did not return, and also to all those who came to our aid in Moray and who never returned to their homelands.

Abstract

At the time of writing there have been many other wars since World War Two, but it is a matter for profound thanks that none of them have been so widespread as to justify the name 'world-wide'. The period covered by the British involvement in the conflict under study was from 3rd September 1939 until the end of the war in Europe on 8th May 1945, and in the Far East on 2nd September 1945 when the war ended with. the surrender of Japan.

The six years of war had a widespread and long lasting effect on Britain. This paper will attempt to set down as much as possible for the record about the involvement of Moray whilst there is still some tangible evidence remaining and whilst there are still some people who can testify from their own experience to the response of this part of Scotland to the call to arms.

Contents

Lists of Illustrations and Appendices

Acknowledgements

Preface

Foreword

Introduction

Part One: Maritime   **page 15**

The Royal Navy RNR RNVR and the WRNS
The Merchant Marine
H M Coast Guard

Part Two: Military   **page 27**

The Regular Army
The Territorial Army and the ATS
The Home Guard and Women's Home Guard
The British Resistance and Auxiliary Signals

Part Three: Air   **page 63**

The Royal Air Force and WAAF
The Air / Sea Rescue Service and RDF

Part Four: Defensive Measures   **page 87**

Part Five: Allies   **page 95**

Polish, Norwegian, American and Canadian
Airmen and Indian

Part Six: Military Administration   **page 107**

Camps and Accommodation.
Prisoners of War

Part Seven: Ag & Fish
page 117

Farming and Fishing
The Women's Land Army and Timber Corps

Part Eight: Medical
page 123

Doctors and Nurses - Red Cross VAD FANYs
Ambulances

Part Nine: Civil Defence
page 129

ARP and AFS
WRVS and Church of Scotland Canteens

Part Ten: Civil Administration
page 139

The Home Front and The Black Out
Rationing - Food, Petrol and Clothing
Evacuation and Identity Cards
Entertainment
Crime and Punishment.
Bombing
Conscription and Conscientious Objectors
Consequences and Casualties
Local Heroes

Part Eleven: Movement Control and Travel
page 161

Restricted Areas and Security
Internment of Aliens
Enemy Agents

Conclusion

Bibliography

Appendices

About the Authors
(back cover)

List of Illustrations:

1   German Invasion Plan
2   The 'Peace Offer' Leaflet
3   Buckie Examination Boat
4   Hopeman Boats
5   Lossiemouth Boats
6   Burghead Boats
7   A Coastguard Post
8   A Bomb Disposal Squad in action
9   Scottish Horsemen
10 Plan of the British Sector for Overlord
11 Pitgaveny Memorial Stone
12 Gow's Castle
13 Miss G Browse and Miss M Farquhar
14 Blairmore House
15 Spigot mortar baseplate
16 A security poster
17 Map of RAF stations
18 20 OTU crest
19 Wellington X
20 RORC instrument
21 Underground bunker
22 Identity card
23 Radar tower
24 Coastal battery
25 Typical armament
26 Anti tank defences
27 Pillbox
28 Holly's seat
29 Dallachy Monument
30 Pinefield Camp
31 Pinefield Hut
32 Training staff camp
33 Former bridging store
34 Pontoon bridge
35 Pontoon raft
36 SBG on tank
37 AVRE
38 LCTs
39 PoW Camp Logie
40 German PoWs
41 WLA poster
42 Red Cross parade
43 ARP poster

44 ARP notice
45 Anderson shelter
46 Sandbags at Leanchoil
47 NFS at Marywell
48 Mobile canteen
49 Ration book
50 Make do and mend poster
51 Evacuees poster
52 ID card
53 Careless talk poster
54 Arandora Star
55 Careless talk poster
56 Portgordon Station
57 BUF at Nuremberg
58 Notice of meeting
59 Monty on R. Findhorn
60 JON cartoon
61 Two types
62 War graves

List of Appendices:

1   Invasion Notice

2   Map of Black Friday

3   Nominal Roll of Auxiliary Home Guard

4   The Blacker Bombard mortar

5   Training and Target beaches compared

6   Recipe for Lord Woolton Pie

7   Agents in training

Acknowledgements

The authors both served in the Army and the Royal Air Force respectively during the Hitlerian unpleasantness and have a nodding acquaintance with most of the material in Parts Two and Three. All the rest, however, is the result of research with many individuals and institutions to whom and to which many thanks are due for their assistance and amongst whom those listed below are included. If there should be any inadvertent omissions it is hoped that sincere apologies will be acceptable.

The authors acknowledge with thanks the information derived, with permission, from Moray Society's lectures given in Elgin Town Hall in 1990 by, amongst others, Mrs Phyllis Anderson, Gp.Capt C Birks RAF, Dr J C M MacDonald and the late Mr C B Wilken. The Authors also participated.

It will be appreciated that though much of the material herein is over sixty years old every effort has been made to locate copyright holders where relevant, but if any are omitted the authors will be pleased to make amends in future editions.

Mrs Phyllis Anderson
Alford Heritage Centre

J. Birnie
J. Brand
Laurence Brander
P. Brett
Miss Margaret Brodie
Mrs Nan Brotchie
Buckie District Fishing Heritage Museum

Mario Cabrelli
Mitchell Campbell
Roger Carr
Mrs Chiappa

Defence of Britain Project
Miss A.J. Denoon (for research in PRO Kew)
Alexander A. Dunbar for permission to use extracts from
J. Brander-Dunbar's diaries
Mrs S. Dunbar for Lord Woolton's recipe
L. Dunbar

Jim Earle (Defence of Britain Project)
A. Ellis H.M.C.G.
Elgin Heritage Centre

Elgin Library

Alan Falconer
D. Fletcher (The Tank Museum)
Allan Fraser
Alex Fraser
R.A. Fresson

Dr Helen Gammie
Archie Gill
A. Granitza
H.M.S.O. Norwich
Dr D. Henderson
Mrs Roma Hossack

Imperial War Museum for permission to use Crown Copyright photos.

Lt. Col. G.S. Johnston OBE. TD. DL. CA.
Mrs S.P. Jones

Kirkwall Library

Dr J.C.M. MacDonald for reading the MSS and for making
many necessary corrections and helpful suggestions.

Greg MacAulay
Mrs M. McColville
George McKay
H. Mackellar
Charlie Mackenzie
John E. Mackenzie
Robin R. Mackenzie
Lt. Col. C. Messenger
John Miele
Dick Milne
Mrs Molly Milne
Ms A. Mitchell
J.G. Rhynas Mitchell
David Morgan
Jim Morrison
Hamish Mustard
Sandy Mutch

Mrs O. O'Callaghan
J. Pieri
Mrs D. Proctor

R.C.A.H.M.S. Edinburgh
George Reid
Dr Peter Reid
Alan Rose

Sandy Scott
Dr Mora Scott MBE. DL.
Mrs Neddy Smith
I.J. Stuart
Paul Sturn (P R O. Kew)
G. Sutherland

The Tank Museum, Bovington
A. Taylor
Mrs H. Tennant
Sir Iain Tennant K.T. for contributing the Foreword.
Geo Townes

Ms S. Usmani

Dr W. Ward (Defence of Britain project)
Elsie and Bob Whyte
John Whyte
C.B. Wilken MBE. TD.
Jack Wood for assistance with graphics.

Mrs M. Yool
Dr N. Young (Imperial War Museum)

Finally, the Authors accept responsibility
for any errors and omissions.

Preface

The aim of this account is to gather, examine and evaluate the significance of all remaining evidence about the involvement of the county of Morayshire during World War Two and the changes it brought about in the lives of the people. The object is to prepare a lasting and comprehensive account for deposition in the record with the Moray Libraries, the Elgin Museum and the Royal Commission on the Ancient and Historic monuments of Scotland in Edinburgh. The method will be to seek out all available remaining evidence of the structures or artefacts associated with the wartime effort that took place between the outbreak of hostilities in 1939 until the end of the war in 1945. It is anticipated that mainly owing to the lapse of more than sixty years, since the war began, that the evidence will be scanty.

Unfortunately many of those involved in the struggle are now beyond our reach but the few remaining survivors will be sought for their contribution. Equally the records of events will be hard to find. Not only were the events often shrouded in secrecy at the time but much of what was recorded, scanty though it may have been, has now been shredded as being of no interest at the present day.

General information about the three armed forces is already well recorded but it does not relate closely to the personal experiences of the people involved. It is hoped that it may be possible to focus the reader's attention more sharply on the personal aspect of the war experience. Equally there were many activities that do not appear to have been at all widely known and some indeed that were actually covert and hidden deep behind a heavy security blanket. After the lapse of time some of these secrets can now be revealed and proper acknowledgement can be made for the bravery and self-sacrifice of the men and women involved.

This work has become a 'portrait of an era', and has swollen to significant proportions in an effort to paint a picture that makes sense to coming generations by recounting some of the outstanding events and conditions that obtained during those turbulent years of upheaval. In spite of its omnibus title there may not have been the residual data to do justice to some aspects of the War in Moray whereas other events, more fully recorded or recalled, may have been dealt with in some detail but this should not be taken to mean that they are of greater significance than those mentioned more succinctly.

For much of the background material necessary to set the chronological scene it has been necessary to some extent to rely on the research of others as the bibliography clearly demonstrates; but so far as possible the authors have confined themselves to original research amongst the surviving sources, both actual and verbal.

Foreword

From Sir Iain Tennant, K.T.

I am sitting on the banks of a Highland Loch idly watching two swans drifting by as the evening sun goes down beyond the hills, all is quiet and peaceful in the countryside. It is the summer of 1939. Little did anyone guess that this peaceful scenario beside the Loch was to be wrecked by nissen huts and tents and troops of all sorts having come together within the past few months to help halt the invader from across the channel.

This is the story of the people of one small county, Moray, who, like other counties of Britain, buried all differences and went to war to preserve peace. Bill Bartlam and Ian Keillar have teamed up to record the events of those days in Moray. They have taken immense trouble with their research as will be seen from the size of the bibliography and they have managed to produce not only a most readable document but one which will be of use to librarians and other authoritarians for generations to come. For my part, I am most grateful and honoured to have been invited to write a Foreword to the work and wish it the wide readership it most richly deserves...

... I see the swans are floating past the lawn once more. This is what we all fought for.

Introduction

Reading, writing and researching about the war brings back memories, not necessarily about past horrors, but of so many odds and ends, many of which merit a paragraph or even a sentence, but which, in total perhaps give more of a flavour of these times than the measured prose and lengthy articles elsewhere.

The country had been prepared for war, but certainly not ready for it, when in 1938 Prime Minister Chamberlain flew to Munich to see Hitler and returned with his famous piece of paper on 30th September. The euphoria of the reprieve evaporated on 15th March 1939 when Germany took over what was left of Czechoslovakia. The slide to war accelerated.

In Moray, most fortuitously, the new wing to Dr. Gray's hospital was opened on Wednesday the 31st of May 1939 but not so happy was the joint exercise of the ARP and the Elgin Fire Brigade, which resulted in the Fire Brigade being strongly criticised. Later, after the start of the war, the Brigade took over an hour to reach a fire at Wester Manbeen, but they did manage to arrive eventually with their new Coventry Climax trailer pump.

Despite preparations for war, domestic activities took up most of the citizen's energies in 1939. There was opposition to a proposed by-pass of Elgin with its "Threat to the Tourist Trade" and on 29th July there were heavy showers of rain and a small amount of snow fell. On Tuesday 1st August, as recounted elsewhere, two aircraft collided near the Boar's Head rock, killing Flying Officer E.W.Yates from Australia as well as two airmen from this country. Their deaths presaged the norm for the next six years.

On the 22nd of August 1939 the world was astounded to hear that the two arch enemies, the Communist Soviet Union and Nazi Germany had signed a non-aggression pact. A war in Europe was now inevitable and on 1st September German tanks crossed into Poland. France and Britain were obliged by treaty to go to the aid of Poland but both countries, still mourning the dead of an earlier war, were reluctant to engage in another; particularly as the Poles were completely unrealistic in their expectations. Negotiations with Hitler continued through the good offices of Sweden's Birger Dahlerus, but Hitler was in no mood for compromise. The French were all for compromise, any compromise which would postpone the evil day, but eventually they agreed with Britain to issue an ultimatum to Germany that she must withdraw all her troops from Poland by 11am (noon in Berlin) on Sunday 3rd September. The deadline came and was ignored by Germany, which was having a short jolly war. Chamberlain, the Prime Minister, came on the wireless to announce lugubriously, 'It is evil things that we shall be fighting against.'

WORLD WAR II IN MORAY

When the war eventually started on Sunday 3rd September 1939 at 11a.m. there was no euphoria as had welcomed the start of the First World War. The army reservists had gone and the newly recruited ARP wardens and Observer Corps took up their positions. In Elgin the Rev. Macdonald of the High Church wrote a strong letter to the 'Northern Scot' complaining that the ARP wardens carried out an exercise on a Sunday, pointing out that there were six other days in which to carry out their activities. Within three weeks, there was an announcement in the same paper that Registration and the issue of Ration Cards would commence shortly.

World War 2 affected everybody in Moray. Although the civilians were not subjected to the bombing inflicted elsewhere, nor to the horrors experienced by many of the inhabitants of Europe, Russia and the Far East, yet the domestic upheavals, the privation, the all encompassing blackout, the influx of service personnel, and the early fear of invasion all contributed to massive changes, both temporary and permanent, in the working patterns and lives of the population.

Churchill, the bungler of Gallipoli and thorn in the side of both Labour and his own nominal party the Conservatives, was brought into the Admiralty. There he exasperated his enemies and exhausted his friends with his enthusiasm for 'action this day'. Meanwhile, in the East, the romantic and gallant Polish cavalry was rapidly turned into horse meat by the German tanks and then, on the 17th September, the treacherous Soviet Union, unctuously preaching about the brotherhood of man, attacked the Poles from the rear and seized about half of their country.

The wartime dictatorship entrusted to Churchill by Parliament after the appeasers and the braggarts had failed to stem the Nazi progress, met Hitler's daring with daring equally ruthless. There is little doubt that Britain's claim to Churchill's gratitude is that although he had dictatorial powers in the conduct of the war, he refused to be one and showed a profound respect for the nation's parliamentary system.

While the German army was busy in the East, there was a time when resolute action by France and Britain could have perhaps the tipped the balance. But the French army was designed to fight a defensive war while the four British divisions in France were too few and too badly equipped to have been of much use in an offensive. Britain, France and Germany settled down to what became known as 'the phony war.' Phony it may have been for many but for some it was real and tragic. In October the mighty warship *Royal Oak* was torpedoed in the allegedly safe harbour of Scapa Flow. In November the Soviet Union attacked Finland and Churchill, no lover of the Soviet Union, proposed that a British expeditionary force be sent, via North Norway, to help the beleaguered

Finns. In February, a British destroyer violated Norwegian territorial waters to release British seamen imprisoned on a German ship, the *S S Altmark* and, emboldened by the success of this operation the British were just about to take on the Soviet Union, as well as Germany, when the Finns capitulated on March 13th 1940, thus saving Britain from absolute disaster.

Meanwhile the Germans had got wind of the British proposals to invade Norway and the definite British intention to mine Norwegian coastal waters on 8th April so, moving quickly, the Germans invaded Denmark and Norway on the 9th April. On 12th April, a hastily reassembled British brigade was dispatched to seize Narvik, and confusion reigned in the British command. Churchill intervened in War Office decisions, while General Ironside, Chief of the Imperial General Staff, fumed as he was over-ruled by a politician. The war in Norway went badly and eventually all British and as many Norwegian troops as possible were evacuated early in June 1940.

While the debacle in Norway was at its height, Parliament debated the situation and by the 8th May Chamberlain was considering resigning. On the 10th May the Germans attacked all along the Western Front, Chamberlain resigned and, after much back room manoeuvering, Churchill became Prime Minister. As Liddell Hart wrote, 'It was the irony, or fatality of history that Churchill should have gained his opportunity of supreme power as the result of a fiasco (Norway) to which he had been the main contributor.' On the 10th of June, Italy, dragging its reluctant colonies of Libya and Abyssinia behind it, entered the war on the side of Germany.

On 16 July 1940 Hitler issued his **Directive No 16, Preparations for a Landing Operation against England.** At the same time Hitler made his 'Last appeal to Reason'. Which was not so much rejected as ignored. Churchill said to his staff, 'I do not propose to say anything in reply to Herr Hitler's speech, not being on speaking terms with him' In Europe, the British Expeditionary Force, now expanded to ten fighting divisions with another three in the rear, in alliance with the French, Belgium and Dutch armies faced 136 German divisions.

In discussing divisions it is important to note that one is not comparing like with like. Although both German and British divisions were units comprising infantry and artillery, engineers and signallers etc. the nominal strength of a British Division was 18,000 while that of a German was 15,100. However, these were very nominal figures and immediately a division went into action its nominal manpower suffered from attrition.

The Dutch army gave in after only 5 days, the Belgian Army surrendered after fighting for 17 days leaving the British flank horribly exposed. On the 26th May, General Gort, the British commander, ordered all his forces to retreat to the Channel ports. For some reason or other the Germans did not take advantage of this tactical advantage and by the 4th of June over 368,000 allied troops had escaped from France through Dunkirk to England, many without their arms and with the loss of the majority of their equipment. They left behind the 51st Highland Division and the 1st Armoured Division and while the 51st was battered into submission at St.Valery the 1st Division retreated west and was eventually rescued from Cherbourg. Paris capitulated on June 14th and Britain expected invasion as soon as the Germans had rested and regrouped.

Churchill, a deplorable strategist and a politically dubious character, rose magnificently to the occasion, and with his determination and oratory he saved Britain. On the 13th of May he told the House of Commons that he had 'nothing to offer save blood, toil, tears and sweat,' and on June 4th, even before France had surrendered, he made the famous broadcast 'We shall fight on the beaches, we shall fight on the landing-grounds, we shall fight in the fields and in the streets, we shall fight in the hills; we shall never surrender'. After the defeat of France, on June 18th, his gravelly bull-dog voice was again on the wireless exhorting his listeners, 'let us brace ourselves to our duty, and so bear ourselves that if the British Empire and its Commonwealth last for a thousand years men will still say, this was their finest hour'.

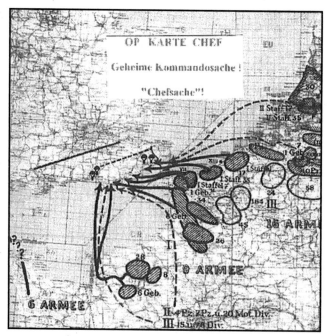

Fig 1. Army Gp 'A Plan
of Sealion' Sept 1940
From Fleming 1957

INTRODUCTION

In Moray, as elsewhere in the country, young men were being called up, the Local Defence Volunteers marched about, fishing boats were converted into mine-sweepers and thousands of tons of concrete were laid down as runways, tank traps and pill-boxes. Children who had been evacuated from the towns at the start of the war and had returned home were once more sent into the country. Country houses were turned into hospitals or military headquarters and troops speaking strange tongues arrived. Canadians came and chopped down trees and, like an oppressive blanket over all was the omnipresent fear of invasion.

As summer turned into autumn the German Luftwaffe started to bomb Britain. At first they targeted the RAF airfields in the south of England and had almost succeeded in neutralising them when they switched tactics and started to bomb cities, principally London. Moray, which had started the war as a safe rural backwater, now found itself within reach of German planes stationed in Norway and, with its wide sandy beaches, was a possible target for invasion. Concrete blocks, backed up by pillboxes, were hurriedly erected along the coast while forests of chopped down trees sprouted along the sands. These were to deter any aircraft from landing on the beaches.

Meanwhile, in the Atlantic there was a continuing battle against the submarines, which threatened to cut off the absolutely essential supplies, which were coming in to Britain, mainly from the U.S.A. In these days of North Sea oil it is difficult to visualise a time when practically every drop of petrol was imported from abroad. But the oil and other supplies had to be paid for and very soon Britain had exhausted all her financial resources. Food, which had been rationed since January 1940 was further reduced later that year and meat, which had been supplied at the rate of 10p per person per week was cut to 5p's worth in 1941.

In May 1941, the mighty battle cruiser, *Hood*, was destroyed off Iceland by the even mightier *Bismarck*, which, in turn was sent to the bottom by torpedoes dropped by obsolete British aircraft. In North Africa General Wavell took the offensive as, almost simultaneously, Italy attacked Greece from its bases in occupied Albania.

By January 1941, British forces had advanced far into Libya and had occupied Tobruk. Meanwhile the Italian offensive against Greece was meeting stiff resistance so Hitler sent German troops into Greece. Britain made a grave strategic blunder when it diverted troops from North Africa to meet the Germans in Greece. Not only were the gains in Libya all lost but the troops sent to Greece were forced to withdraw to Crete with the loss of most of their heavy equipment. The Germans attacked Crete on the 20th May mainly using parachutists. These elite troops suffered terrible casualties but eventually captured the island.

In Iraq, a local warlord, Raschid Ali, attacked Britain's great air base at Habbanyia outside Baghdad and threatened Britain's vital oil supply in the Gulf. Few troops could be spared to go to the defence of Habbanyia but the Air Force exchanged their spanners for rifles and beat off the attackers. Elsewhere in the Middle East, General Wavell was ordered by Churchill to occupy Syria and, almost simultaneously, attack once again in Libya. The Libyan campaign was a disaster and Churchill blamed Wavell who was replaced by Auchinleck.

And then on 22nd June Hitler made the strategic error of opening a second front, when from the Baltic to the Black Sea, German troops with their allies, invaded the Soviet Union. Churchill welcomed his new friends with the words ' If Hitler invaded Hell I would at least make a favourable mention of the Devil in the House of Commons'.

At first all went well for the Germans. Soviet armies were destroyed or rounded up as the armoured divisions of the Reich stormed on to Leningrad, Moscow and the Crimea. But the diversions in the Balkans and Greece had taken up valuable time and before the German armies could sweep into their intended destinations, General Winter counter attacked. The snow came early in 1941 and the cold with it was intense. The German soldiers were not equipped for winter warfare and suffered terribly. The winter gave time for the Soviets to train and equip new troops for the next year. In Britain the realisation of Soviet weakness and probable early defeat increased the fear and awareness of a subsequent German invasion and counter preparations had to be 'at concert pitch' by the 1st September 1941. The Home Guard, the renamed L.D.V. or Local Defence Volunteers, endured more realistic training and were equipped with more effective weapons such as mortars

Post-war research points to the conclusion that Hitler was reluctant to involve Britain in a conflict if he could possibly achieve his aims by other means. He clung to the illusion that the British would not fight and made several increasingly desperate threats followed by 'appeals to reason', all of which were studiously ignored by Churchill. Finally on the night 1/2 August the Luftwaffe dropped leaflets over various parts of England with Hitler's 'Last Appeal to Reason,' being a translation of the 'peace offer leaflet' he had made in a Reichstag speech nearly two weeks earlier. On 3rd August H M The King of Sweden offered to

Fig 2. The 'peace Offer'
Photo: Daily Graphic

act as mediator. None of these offers was accepted, in fact the whole bizarre affair made no sense and was therefore treated as risible.

But 1941 had not yet finished with its alarms and excursions. In the Far East, Japan had been flexing its muscles; first by conquering Manchuria and then by invading China. The U.S.A. tried to control the situation by denying Japan access to oil. Japan responded by the memorable attack on the American Fleet at Pearl Harbour on 7th December, 'the day of infamy' and simultaneous attacks on Hong Kong, Malaya and the Dutch East Indies, now Indonesia. Four days after the initial Japanese attack, the British Navy suffered a humiliating and salutary defeat when aircraft sank the battleships *Repulse* and *Prince of Wales* off the coast of Malaya. From that dark day onwards the Navy accepted that aircraft could sink warships.

In Malaya, Japanese soldiers moved down the peninsula to Singapore 'the lion of the east' while elsewhere in the region their murderous troops swarmed all over, causing the British to retreat from Burma across the unforgiving mountains into India. Christmas Day 1941 saw the surrender of Hong Kong, followed by an orgiastic massacre of several of the defenders. As the winter of 1941 slipped into the spring of 1942 it would be pleasing to say that Singapore fought gallantly to the end. But this would be a travesty of the truth. Despite General Percival having some three times more troops than his Japanese opponent, after only seven days of fighting, on the 15th of February, Percival asked for and received permission from London to surrender.

About 140,000 allied troops were killed or captured in Malaya and Singapore and many of those who surrendered would lose their lives on the infamous Burma railroad. With the summer of 1942 the Japanese had conquered practically all of Asia beyond India and Ceylon. The German armies recommenced their advance and rolled down to the Volga and the great city of Stalingrad. In Egypt, Rommel, the charismatic and popular German general, had advanced as far as Alamein some 60 miles (100km) from Alexandria. In Australia, the harsh reality was that no longer could the British Navy protect their shores and the country was now dependent for its security upon the United States.

1942 started badly for the Allies but by the New Year of 1943 there was more than a glimmer of hope on the horizon. Despite the efforts of the German armies the key cities of Leningrand, Moscow and Stalingrad still remained under Soviet control. Leningrad was held tight in a merciless siege while Stalingrad was reduced to rubble but still held out, and Moscow had pushed the enemy a little bit further away from the city. In Egypt the British 8th army destroyed Rommel's forces and, in Britain, church bells were rung for this small but significant victory. Also in Britain, the build-up of the Air Force was starting to show results and Air Marshal Arthur Harris, 'Bomber Harris' to the public and 'Butcher Harris' to his crews yet idolised by them, mounted a thousand bomber raid on Cologne in May 1942.

After the harsh winters of the early war years the winter of 1942/43 was mild, but this did not prevent the surrender of the whole of the German 6th army at Stalingrad early in February 1943 when almost a quarter of a million men were lost. In North Africa the advancing 8th army met up with Americans and the British 1st Army in Tunisia and there took the surrender of a quarter of a million enemy soldiers. Oblivious to German losses, Hitler planned a great set piece battle at Kursk for the summer of 1943. Guns and new tanks were transported to the East and in July a terrible battle erupted in the Steppes. The Germans had a technological superiority but the Russians had an overwhelming manpower advantage. Wave after wave of infantry flung themselves upon the German machine gunners. As the guns heated there was no time to change barrels so the Russians charged to victory over the bodies of their own dead. After Kursk the mighty Wehrmacht was in continuos retreat.

Simultaneously, as the slaughter continued in Russia, the allies invaded Sicily and then pushed on into Italy proper. On July 25th, Mussolini, dictator of Italy, was dismissed by the king and Italians in Britain, until then treated as prisoners-of-war, were reclassified as co-combatants, as the Germans, once their allies, now treated their one-time comrades as enemies. As allied troops painfully battled their way up the spine of Italy and Russia started to advance westwards the Americans started the long slow progress of island hopping with Japan as their final destination. In Britain, planning and preparation for a proposed invasion of Europe was started.

By the winter of 1943/44 Bomber Command was building up to the frightening force, which it was soon to become. Large four engined bombers such as the Lancaster and the Halifax were now on all squadrons and practically every night some German city was subjected to terrifying raids. As Harris said 'The Germans sowed the wind and now they must reap the whirlwind'. And what a whirlwind they reaped. Hamburg was subjected to a firestorm in August 1943 while Berlin was regularly bombed all through that winter.

In 1944 the Japanese had followed the retreating British from Burma to Imphal and Kohima in India but unlike the British they took with them mortars and artillery complete with ammunition. This was one of the greatest feats of the war and even if carried out by a cruel and ruthless enemy it illustrates what mankind is capable of doing, even for an unworthy cause. In the spring of 1944 the Japanese launched fierce attacks on Imphal and Kohima. The British troops were surrounded but were supplied by parachuted supplies carried by the ubiquitous DC3 or Dakota. The starving Japanese launched attack after attack but were eventually broken and retreated in defeat. General Slim, in command of the 14th (forgotten) Army, after regrouping and resting his troops, then pursued the Japanese down into Burma.

Despite the fact that the Soviet Red Army was advancing towards the west, the Nazis continued with their systematic massacre of European Jews and others whom they considered as undesirables. As German troops waited desperately for ammunition, trains were being diverted to trundle men, women and children into extermination camps. Some six million Jews and many others were systematically murdered in camps scattered throughout Eastern Europe.

In Britain, war weariness was becoming evident and the crime rate was rising, always a good inverse barometer of social coherence. However, there was urgent work to be done in preparing for the invasion of Europe and the opening of the long awaited second front. In Moray there were rehearsals off the coast while Southern England was turned into a vast military camp and vehicle park. All military leave was stopped to minimise the danger that careless talk could cost lives. General Eisenhower was placed in overall command with General Montgomery, the victor at Alamein, as his second in command. Their relationship was not a happy one.

The invasion, operation OVERLORD, took place on June 6th 1944 when a great armada of ships landed in that first bloody day some 156,000 troops on the beaches of Normandy. The allies were helped considerably by Hitler taking tactical control of the German forces. He was convinced that the attack on Normandy was a feint and that the main attack would occur near Calais. As Hitler bacame even more maniacal he replaced Field Marshal von Runstedt with von Kluge, who in turn was superseded by Field Marshal Model when Kluge committed suicide. By August 24th the Americans were in Paris, although for political reasons it was allowed to appear that the French liberated the city on the 25th. In Italy, Rome had fallen to the allies while in the east the Red Army continued its remorseless path westward.

In the Pacific, the Americans continued their island hopping towards Japan and when they took Saipan, after ferocious fighting in June 1944 when 19,000 Japanese were killed for the loss of 15,000 American marines, the cities of Japan were now within range of allied bombers. Within a month American bombers were attacking mainland Japan and the loss of Guam by 10th August tightened the noose around the country of the rising sun.

On 13th June 1944 the Germans launched the first pilotless planes or doodle-bugs towards London. These flying bombs had a crude jet engine, which cut out at a predetermined point and the whole contraption then fell to earth, detonating when it hit the ground. So long as you could hear the put-put of the engine you were quite safe, but when the engine stopped you knew that you had only a few seconds before the explosion would occur. Later on, in the autumn the Germans fired rockets, the V2, which arrived without warning but detonated with a distinctive double explosion.

On 20th August, in the 'wolf's lair' in Poland, several German officers tried to assassinate Hitler. Unfortunately, the attempt failed and Hitler took a terrible revenge, both against the actual plotters and those who were just suspected of being involved. Many distinguished officers, including those who had fought gallantly with the forces, were strung up on piano wire attached to meat hooks. Hitler had their death throes captured on film so that he could gloat over their fate in private. Rommel, one of the alleged conspirators, was too great a hero to be murdered, so he was allowed to take poison and was then given a magnificent state funeral.

On September 17th the allies launched operation 'Market Garden' in which parachute forces landed deep into Holland in order to establish a bridgehead across the Rhine and hopefully win the war before the winter slowed down operations. The idea was sound but the Germans reacted swiftly and the war was destined to last into another year. As winter closed down operations on the Western Front the allied forces relaxed a little and troops were sent on leave. While home for Christmas was not possible for most, at least it was a possibility for some. The storm broke on December 16th when Von Rundstedt launched a desperate offensive in the Ardennes taking advantage of the snowy, foggy weather. The German drove a wedge some 45 miles (70km) deep into the allied line but the weather cleared on the 22nd December and the allied supremacy in the air resulted in a turkey shoot of the German forces.

The year 1945 was to see the end of this bitter long drawn out war. In Britain there was confidence that Germany would soon be defeated but after that there was talk of another two years to finish off Japan. On the night of 13th to 14th February, the Royal Air Force, in two massive air raids, destroyed the baroque city of Dresden. Dresden was filled with refugees, mainly women and children, and the casualties were uncountable. 27,000 houses and 7,000 public buildings were completely destroyed while 6 square miles (15 sq.km) of the inner city were reduced to rubble. The judgement of Marshal Harris in ordering this attack was a matter of much discussion. Simultaneously attacked from east and west, the German Reich cracked in early May. On April 30th Hitler, besieged in his Berlin bunker, shot himself after nominating Admiral Doenitz as his successor. Doenitz immediately opened negotiations with the allies and on May 7th General Jodl, for the German High Command, signed an instrument of surrender and Britain declared May 8th 1945 as 'VE Day' Victory in Europe.

INTRODUCTION

After jubilation in the cities of the free world, the reality dawned that the war with Japan still raged on. Troops were withdrawn from Europe and after home leave were then being shipped out to the Far East. An invasion of Japan was planned and massive casualties were anticipated as it was expected that the Japanese would fight to the last man, woman and child. Meanwhile the coalition government in Britain fell apart and a general election was called for the 5th July, when Churchill, the architect of victory, was rejected and which the Labour Party won unexpectedly with a handsome majority.

In Japan devastating air raids reduced the country's industrial output. In one air raid on Tokyo in March more people were killed than were lost in the whole of Britain in six years of war and the output from essential war factories was reduced to a quarter of its former peak. The civilian members of the Japanese government were in favour of suing for peace but the military was adamant that they must continue the war. General Marshall advised that an invasion of Japan would cost up to a million casualties and faced with these circumstances, President Truman authorised the use of the newly developed atomic bomb.

The first atomic bomb was dropped on Hiroshima on 6th August and, since the Japanese did not respond immediately a second bomb was dropped on Nagasaki. This had the desired effect. The Japanese immediately sued for peace and accepted the terms offered on August 14th 1945.

The most terrible war in history was now at an end. The troops could return home, but only slowly. Britain had not been invaded but it was a different country to which the servicemen returned. The six years had been hazardous for those sent abroad and difficult and challenging for those left at home and this introduction sets the scene for the story of these years and is a memorial, however imperfect, to all those who did their bit.

**WORLD WAR II
IN MORAY**

PART ONE
Maritime

Part One

Maritime

The Royal Navy, The Royal Naval Reserve and The Royal Naval Volunteer Reserve

With a significant proportion of the population engaged in deep-sea fishing it is not surprising that the Royal Navy had a considerable influence and recruited widely in Morayshire during both World Wars. In fact fishermen of the Moray Firth had been joining the Royal Naval Reserve since 1880; first as seamen but in this century as skippers and skipper Lieutenants. Many more joined after the 1914-18 war when the Royal Naval Patrol Service began. In 1939 with the outbreak of World War Two about half of the fishermen in Lossiemouth, Hopeman and Burghead were in the Royal Naval Reserve and even before war was declared 30 skippers and 60 seamen were called up These men were dispatched for training to the Lowestoft Division of the Royal Navy at HMS Europa, a shore station. By mid 1944 The Royal Navy had 863,500 including 73,500 WRNS.

Shortly after War was declared a large number of fishing boats were taken up for service and prepared for war with the fleets. In Lossiemouth, for example, there were 98 boats registered at Inverness (INS) and 40 were selected. The reduced fishing fleet left to pursue its peace time calling and continued to fish, providing an important part of the restricted and rationed diet enforced throughout the war and for several years afterwards. The boats taken for service with the Royal Navy were stripped of their fishing gear that was eventually used up by the remaining boats, which carried on fishing.

As First Lord of the Admiralty, Winston Churchill foresaw the call up of boats for naval service, as they had been during the first war, and arranged with Ernest Bevin, secretary of the Transport and General Workers' Union to iron out any difficulties there might have been with the Union. The crews of the commandeered boats retained their merchant navy status. The boats were dispersed about a variety of duties. Some went to the large naval bases at Invergordon and Scapa Flow but these postings were by no means all local, some eventually went as far as Malta and even the Far East, for example. In their new stations the boats were used as 'maids of all work', fetching and carrying for the capital ships between their anchorages and the shore bases.

Other fishing boats were engaged on minesweeping, until purpose built minesweepers were available. Some boats were employed on patrol work in the Moray Forth between Kinnaird Head and Duncansby Head. Here they were on the lookout for enemy ships and for mines laid by enemy aircraft. They also performed valuable service by spotting and rescuing downed airmen and reporting downed aircraft. Despite the vigilance of these patrols U-Boats succeeded in sinking the *SS Astronaut*, a tanker of 18,000 tons, in the Firth while another, the *SS Greta Field*, was sunk by bombers off Wick.

The harbours were closed at dusk and three boats were lined up across the harbour mouth with the Examination Boat included in the centre, together with a chain that was stretched across the opening. The three boats were ballasted and prepared for sinking as blockships if the harbour were to be invaded. The fishing fleet operated only in daylight hours with a curfew enforced as well as a statutory radius of operation. Boats that were found at sea outside these restrictions were automatically assumed to be hostile and were liable to be fired upon. The examination boats were modified MFVs with the fish hold converted to accommodation for the Royal Navy crew who lived aboard. All vessels seeking entry to the harbour were supposed to be examined, in fact virtually all the boats were well known to the examination crew, so that in reality they had little to do, except in Buckie which had many refugee boats from Scandinavia.

Fig 3. The Buckie Examination vessel BCK 357
Photo: Buckie District Fishing Heritage Museum

The Buckie examination vessel was a former drifter. She was built in 1904 in Rotterdam for William Smith of Ianstown and was registered as The Swallow BF1539. She measured 81' 5"x 18'.1" with a draught of 8'10". Powered by a 30hp compound engine by Crabtree of Yarmouth she was re-registered in 1920 as BCK 357 for the same owners. She was taken up for war service from 1915 until 1919 and re-named Swallow III. Fitted with a 3 pdr gun she acted as an anti-submarine net vessel and minesweeper. In World War 2 she was again requisitioned as an Examination or Interception vessel and did duty in Buckie harbour where she was also earmarked as a blockship for the harbour entrance. Her machinery was stripped out and sold for scrap in 1952 and the hull, filled with cork, was used as a target ship by the RAF. She was eventually sunk in the Moray Firth in 1956.

Many Lossiemouth fishermen served in the 144th Coastal Services Squadron. This unit was equipped with Motor Launches powered by twin Gardner diesel engines, and which were well armed, especially against air attack. Crews were trained in Lowestoft before sailing to the Mediterranean where they were employed guarding ships in Alexandria harbour from attacks by Italian two-man torpedoes that had been achieving some success by sinking two battleships in December 1941. The squadron achieved some distinction during the invasion of Sicily where it was employed sweeping mines, on anti-aircraft defence as markers for the invasion craft and as rescue vessels.

The Royal Navy also used two-man torpedoes in attacks against the Italian Fleet in Palermo harbour in November 1942. It was here that Lieut Greenland with Leading Signalman Alexander Ferrier, from Elgin, successfully attacked a large Italian Cruiser and were taken prisoner. Sandy Ferrier was awarded the Conspicuous Gallantry Medal for his part in the attack. This award was in addition to the Polish Cross of Valour he had won during the second battle of Narvik in 1940 whilst serving on a Polish Warship. FERRIER TERRACE in Bishopmill, Elgin is so named in his honour. One of the Royal Navy's tasks in the Moray Firth occurred during the winter of 1943 and the spring of 1944 when it took an all important part in the rehearsals for the Normandy landings, codeword Operation OVERLORD. The Naval Task force 'S' was commanded by Rear Admiral Talbert under Vice Admiral Sir Philip Vian of *HMS Cossack* and *SS Altmark* fame, who commanded all the British Naval Forces on 'D' day during the assault on Hitler's 'Fortress Europe'.

The Royal Navy and the WRNS

The WRNS (Women's Royal Naval Service) was formed in 1939 to replace Naval Officers and men on some duties in time of war. They started with a strength of 1,000 but this rapidly increased until by 1945 there were 74,600 serving. There was no established Naval station in Morayshire so these WRNS were only seen when they came home on leave or on some special temporary detachment, as for example on one occasion from Aberdeen to prime depth charges on board minesweepers in Lossiemouth harbour.

The Merchant Marine

As an island nation much of our food and raw materials comes from abroad, including most of our meat, cheese, butter and wheat as well as steel, timber, wool, cotton, nitrates, zinc and lead. British farmers would not have been able to produce their crops without imported fertilisers. Almost all of Britain's oil and petroleum supplies were shipped across the Atlantic.

When Hitler decided on blockading our ports and attacking our merchant fleets with his U-Boats our survival became a matter of grave concern to the Government. It seemed for a while that despite the gallant sacrifices being made by our merchant sailors, who were losing the battle of attrition, with the loss of so many men, ships and cargoes, that it was only a matter of time before we should be forced to surrender to avoid starvation. The end would come when we reached the figure of 600,000 tons of shipping lost each month. In March 1941 Churchill is quoted as saying 'shipping losses (are) the supreme menace of the war'. Yet despite his long experience he was slow to adopt the well tried and successful convoy system. Early in 1941 the average monthly losses were 400,000 tons rising later in April to nearly 700,000 tons and rations were reduced. A J P Taylor called it 'the moment when Great Britain came nearest to losing the war'.

The U-Boats laid siege in the Atlantic and were sinking upwards of half a million tons of shipping monthly. We were losing ships faster than they could be replaced, and tragically with each ship sunk men were also lost. It was not until 1942 that shipbuilders began to overtake the loss rate and by 1945 the merchant fleet had gone from 32 million tons to 54 million tons. As well as losses from U-Boats the introduction of discrete types of sea mines was also accounting for heavy losses. The record shows that in the three months during the winter of 1939-40 losses from magnetic mines totalled a quarter of a million tons of allied shipping.

Equally as hazardous as the Atlantic convoys were the Arctic convoys to Murmansk with material for the Russians who were locked in combat with the Germans, their former allies. The incessant attacks from the German bases in Norway were a problem added to the awful weather conditions in those northern seas where the build up of ice on a ship's superstructure threatened its stability, unless removed by constant attention. The convoys through the Mediterranean to relieve Malta were just as dangerous.

The problems facing the Naval Escorts were various, to begin with there were nothing like enough escort vessels available at the start of the war. The building programme had concentrated on capital ships. The Canadian government decided that their main war effort would be in supplying escort ships and by May

1942 they had produced 300. A further problem was experienced by the fall of France allowing the U-boats to establish bases in the French ports of Lorient, Brest, St Nazaire, and La Rochelle. This cut down the time taken for the enemy to arrive at their Atlantic stations, reducing their turn-round time by 22%. The limited performance of 'Asdic' for detecting U-boats was another problem facing the escorts in hunting the enemy. The equipment was inoperable in rough water, a common occurrence in the Atlantic, or if the vessel was moving in excess of 20 knots it could not penetrate the water layers of different salinity or temperature.

The result of all these factors was loss of life among the merchant seamen. The immediate aid available to civilian casualties ashore was denied the civilian casualties suffered at sea. Usually attacked at night there was no warning and the survivors of the crews, many of whom were not young, were often wounded and found themselves in water that was always cold, rough and even sub-arctic at times. Many of them were bleeding and half drowned, possibly mutilated and abandoned to drift in open boats where many went mad and died of thirst and exposure.

The following lists show the vessels taken up for war service from Hopeman, Lossiemouth and Burghead in 1939-1945.

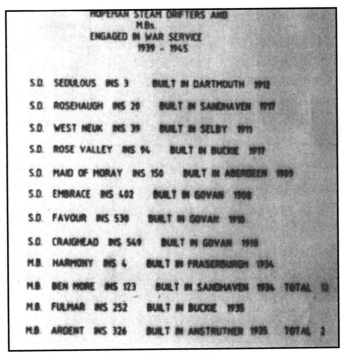

Fig 4. Hopeman boats

LOSSIEMOUTH SEINE NET VESSELS REQUISITIONED 1939 TO 1945

SCAPA FLOW AND OTHER DESTINATIONS.

INS. 35 MORNING STAR	INS. 184 CORNUCOPIA
INS. 37 VICTORY	INS. 196 ATALANTA
INS. 64 KIA-ORA	INS. 225 HELENDALE
INS. 78 MAGGIE COWIE	INS. 251 DAISY
INS. 82 AJAX	INS. 261 THISTLE
INS. 90 VERBENA	INS. 264 SALVIA
INS. 96 VIGILANT	INS. 277 MURIEL
INS. 100 MARGUERITE	INS. 289 MISTLETOE
INS. 103 WINDSOR	INS. 307 COVESEA
INS. 107 WINDSOR LAD	INS. 324 CEDAR
INS. 111 SHANNON	INS. 327 PLOUGH
INS. 134 UNITED	INS. 329 ROSE

LOSSIE STEAM DRIFTERS ON GOVT. SERVICE 1939/1945.

INS. 171 DARNAWAY

INS. 365 DRAINIE

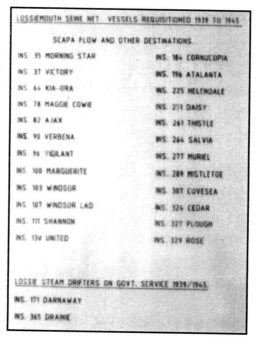

Fig 5. Lossiemouth boats

BURGHEAD BOATS ON GOVT SERVICE 1939/1945

STEAM		MOTOR	
DOORIE BRAE	INS 344	ROSELEA	INS 130
MORAY ROSE	INS 101		
RIANT	INS 30	TOTAL	1
LYDIA LONG	INS 38		
BELLA MORAY	INS 256		
BROCH HEAD	INS 254		
PROVOST	INS 545		
LUCRATIVE	INS 66		
MORAY VIEW	INS 22		
ROSEISLE			
TOTAL	10		

Fig 6. Burghead boats

H M Coastguard

The Coastguard Service Act (1925) still allowed the Admiralty control of the Coastguard in time of national need. In the 1930s the departments (Board of Trade and Admiralty) worked together to prepare the Coastguard as a War Watching Organisation. The basis of the organisation was the maintenance of look-out by the CG stations, War and Port War Signal Stations, to allow warning to be given of the approach of enemy forces or other dangers so that defensive action could be taken. Peace-time duties would continue and some stations would also report movements of enemy aircraft as part of the Air Intelligence Organisation.

When war came 4,500 Auxiliary Coastguards were recruited on National Service to strengthen stations throughout Britain. The twin skills of intelligence gathering and reporting and signalling were of primary importance and in May 1940, as the possibility of invasion loomed ever larger, the Admiralty assumed control and armed the Coastguard service.

As soon as war began Coastguards opened their secret instructions that had been prepared in May 1939, and issued ready for when war was declared. These instructed all stations to assume a constant watch and to report all suspicious vessels, which resulted in a steady stream of information fed back to various control centres.

An inspection of the service by Vice-Admiral R V Holt, acting on instructions from the First Lord of the Admiralty, in 1940 uncovered an unusual group of coast watchers at Golspie, where a Miss Alexandra Sinclair had enlisted a voluntary Corps of Lady Watchers, who were reported as acting most efficiently.

There was close co-operation with the Royal Observer Corps and direct telephone lines were established between ROC posts and CG stations in some areas. This co-operation was particularly helpful in spotting and fixing the position of downed airmen, allowing the Air/Sea Rescue Service to save many lives when the airman baling out of a ditched aircraft could be spotted, and a cross bearing taken allowing the 'crash boats' to locate the casualty with a minimum of delay, particularly important in winter time.

A Defence Regulation assumed the Auxiliaries of the Coastguard Service as Armed Forces of the Crown and they were therefore subject to Naval Discipline whilst on duty and were put on the books of *HMS President II* and ranked as Able Seamen. Moreover they were, from 16 February 1942 dressed in khaki battledress with 'Coastguard' shoulder flashes.(Webb. 1976:119). The traditional badged blue peaked cap was retained. The service was armed with rifles for the defence of their posts against possible saboteurs, and to enable suspected persons to be detained. Sten guns were issued later when they came into general use, some look-out huts also had Thompson sub-machine guns issued.

Fig 7. The CG post at Lossiemouth, now disused.
Photo: W.A.B.

Coastguards were warned to report the sighting of carrier pigeons flying out from the shore as they might be dispatched by enemy agents, but on no account were pigeons to be shot! Courses in aircraft recognition were arranged and reports were required of the numbers and types of enemy aircraft sighted.

Towards the end of 1944 the coastwise War Watch was reduced in intensity and the service was reduced in numbers by some 2,000. On 1 October 1945 the Admiralty reluctantly relinquished control and the service continued to be administered instead by the Ministry of War Transport, later becoming the Ministry of Transport then the Ministry of Transport and Civil Aviation.

It was altogether 19 years before the service finally reverted to control of the Marine Division of the Board of Trade The Auxiliary Coastguard was officially stood down and disbanded on 30 November 1945, and in June 1946 the Coastguard got back its traditional blue uniform.

Altogether, by the end of 1940, there had been 371 stations, 335 coast-watching posts and 199 coast-searching posts. War watching Stations in the Moray area were located at Banff, Portsoy, Cullen, Buckie, Lossiemouth and Burghead. There was no station further west than Burghead on the south shore of the Moray Firth though there were stations on the north shore at Cromarty, Portmahomack and Helmsdale etc. It was realised that these stations covered only the more important points and considerable reliance was also placed on reports from lighthouse keepers.

In the matter of communications it was agreed that the necessary standard of visual signalling could not be expected from the supplementary personnel and reliance was placed on the telephone and radio. There was also a difficulty reported here in that the language of a Buchan or West Coast supplementary was usually incomprehensible to an Englishman, as was the reverse.

Although one of the duties of the War Watchers was to look out for enemy agents landing on our shores they appear to have missed the only three parties that landed in the area. On 30 September 1940 three agents came ashore at Portgordon, on 25 October 1940 three agents came ashore at the Culbin Bar and on April 1941 two agents came ashore at Crovie. The Coastguard was, however successful in recovering the inflatable dinghy as used by the Portgordon spies (see part eleven).

WORLD WAR II
IN MORAY

PART TWO

MILITARY

Part Two

Military

The Regular and the Territorial Armies

The Seaforth Highlanders

Moray is traditionally Mackenzie country, though with strong affiliations to the Gordons, but the local regular army infantry regiment is the Seaforth Highlanders and they wear the Mackenzie tartan. It is a regiment with a proud history and tradition, and supported a Territorial Seaforth Battalion. Most Scottish Counties had Territorial Infantry Battalions that all served throughout the First World War. The 6th Battalion Seaforth Highlanders was the County of Moray's Battalion, the successor to the old Volunteer Battalion.

The Battalion had its Headquarters and 'HQ' and 'A' Companies in Elgin Drill Hall, 'B' Company was in Forres, 'C' Company was in Rothes and 'D' Company was in Grantown. The total strength of the Battalion was about 600 Officers, NCO's and Men. As was usual in the Territorial Army the Adjutant, Quartermaster, Regimental Sergeant Major and Sergeant Instructors, one to each Company, were all Regular Army. Most Territorial Battalions were mobilised shortly prior to the outbreak of war and 6th Seaforth was mobilised on 30th August 1939 just four days before war was declared.

In October the Battalion was ordered to move to Aldershot where it joined the 51st Highland Division. Then in January 1940 it sailed for France as part of the British Expeditionary Force. After only a few weeks in France the 6th Battalion was transferred to 5th Division, being replaced in the 51st Division by 2nd Battalion Seaforth. This was a lucky move for the 6th Battalion as if it had remained with the 51st Division it would have gone into captivity at St Valery in June 1940. As it was the transfer to 5th Division was the beginning of a long journey that eventually took the Battalion from France to Belgium and Dunkirk, thence back to the UK and then Northern Ireland, South of England, Madagascar, India, Iran, Iraq, Egypt, Palestine, Sicily, Italy and finally to Germany and the end of the war. Like the 6th Battalion Seaforth the 7th Battalion served throughout the First World War with distinction. In 1939 the Battalion was stationed at Forres where it mobilised on 4th September. It recruited initially from Morayshire and absorbed surplus numbers from the 6th Battalion. One of the immediate duties that fell to the Battalion was to provide guards for vulnerable points in the district at places like RAF stations at Kinloss and Lossiemouth, the BBC station at Burghead and the railway viaducts at Tomatin and Culloden, despite their being in Cameron country. Inevitably, the question was asked, 'why can't the Camerons guard their own vulnerable points?'

Although the Battalion had no less than seven schoolmasters among these officers the unit was under strength, and recruited from Fort George and from some north of England Regular units. Moving in late spring of 1940 to Tain more recruits were enlisted, including some from London who are reported to have been mystified by the prevailing accents but impressed by the scenery. Due to its proximity to the Navy's Oil Tank Farm at Invergordon, Tain was a special security area and the Battalion was located under canvas at Tarlogie Wood near to Glenmorangie Distillery, which was unfortunately closed down for the 'duration'.

In October 1940 the Battalion was embarked for Shetland being bombed for the first time whilst on passage. No casualties were sustained but the unit's Ack-Ack Bren gunners took the opportunity to open fire on the enemy for the first time-unsuccessfully. With the Germans in strength in Norway, Shetland had been turned into a fortress, as it lay nearer to Norway than it did to Scotland. Whilst in Shetland for 13 months they had extremes of weather and the first wartime casualties were experienced during an air-raid when a Sergeant was killed and three men were wounded.

In Autumn 1941 the Battalion moved into Northumberland and came under command of the 46th Highland Brigade, part of 15th Scottish Infantry Division with which the battalion served until demobilisation at the end of 1945. After extensive training with other arms the 15th Scottish Division crossed over into Normandy in mid June 1944 and was almost continually in action until the cessation of hostilities on 5th May 1945.

The unit formed part of the army of occupation until eventually disbanding in December 1945

The Royal Engineers

The Royal Engineers had a particularly close connection with Morayshire for two main reasons. First, because Pinefield Camp, at Elgin, was occupied by the regiment during most of the war up to 1943 and the approach of the Normandy invasion. Associated training areas were used by the regiment to learn and practise its arcane skills, like bridging, at the former Gilston Loch, pontoon bridging and rafting at Findhorn and demolitions and explosives north of Elgin at Woodside. In the run up to 'D day' 5 Assault Regiment RE, equipped with Churchill tanks, was stationed at Fort George but carried out, in the four winter months, no less than seven full scale exercises involving frequent assault landings on the beaches west of Burghead with supporting arms and using live ammunition. When the exercises were over the tanks made their way back by road to Fort George. As the winter of 1943-4 was quite severe the roads were frequently icy or snowbound leading to much loss of directional control and consequent damage to roadside hedges, fences and telegraph poles.

During the exercise and immediately prior to the landings the beach area was subject to carpet bombing from rocket firing ships. Owing to the soft nature of the ground in the Culbin Sands area many of the bombs failed to explode and this is the second reason why the Royal Engineers had such a close connection with Morayshire. They provided Bomb Disposal teams equipped with army vehicles carrying the letters BDS and with their mudguards and bumpers painted red.

The UXB, or unexploded bomb, was a particular hazard that became apparent early in the war when the Nazis began air raids over our cities. Delay action bombs were mixed in with active bombs to cause maximum disruption to wartime production and civilian morale. No preparations had been made by the Government before the war for such an eventuality, despite the earlier appearance of this type of warfare in Spain during the civil war in 1936, and early in 1940 the responsibility for bomb disposal was passed to the Royal Engineers to form Bomb Disposal units. It was an extremely dangerous and stressful job for which the life expectancy was reckoned at a maximum of 10 weeks. The work demanded a rare and high form of courage to deal in cold blood with a deadly monster that could at any moment explode and wipe you out. The delay action fuse was invented and developed in 1932. A clockwork mechanism could be set to delay the explosion for up to 72 hours.

It was not until a bomb was successfully recovered intact that a clock stopping equipment was developed. Soon, anti-handling booby traps were added and so on until the devices were practically impossible to neutralise. It was only when the occasional bomb was

Fig 8. BD squad defusing a 12,000lb bomb
From Fleming 1957

recovered intact and new fuses were analysed that it was possible to bridge gaps in the RE knowledge. Fortunately few, if any, DA bombs were dropped in Morayshire. In fact the pattern of bombing was so slight by comparison with elsewhere that it even seemed it may have been caused by enemy returning home without having been able to deliver their total bomb load on the main target and simply dumping them on targets of opportunity before they crossed the coast. This compares with 1,500 UXBs on London in the first week of December 1940.

The clearance of land mines was done by all combat troops, particularly by the infantry, although in special circumstances, such as before a major operation, approach lanes would often be cleared by special mine clearance RE teams ahead of the advance. The responsibility for dealing with sea mines fell on the men of Royal Navy who were equally heroic in dealing with the huge mines dropped by parachute and which were almost always booby trapped with anti-handling devices.

The Scottish Horse

The Scottish Horse is a comparatively young Regiment. It was founded in South Africa in 1900 as mounted infantry of Scots descent. Lord Tullibardine, later to become the 8th Duke of Atholl, was commissioned as a result of his service with Kitchener in the Sudan, to raise two regiments, one in Perthshire and one in North East Scotland. In the First World War the Scottish Horse fought at Gallipoli and was reformed after the war as a mounted unit, the men wearing the Atholl Bonnet.

At the outbreak of World War Two the Regiment was mobilised at Dunkeld on 2nd September 1939, and the Elgin contingent left Elgin for Dunkeld by rail. At the end of 1939 the policy decision was taken to convert the Regiment into an artillery role. And in April 1940 the Scottish Horse became the 19th and 80th, Morayshire contingent, (Scottish Horse) Medium Regiment Royal

Fig 9. A youthful Hamish Proctor and Sandy Chalmers in the uniform of the Scottish Horse.

Photo: Courtesy Alex Fraser

Artillery. The Atholl Bonnet and the Scottish Horse cap badge were retained. After prolonged training in their new role the Regiment was mobilised in December 1942 for overseas service. And on 21st February 1943 they sailed from the Clyde for Durban and the country of their origin. In July they were placed in support of 51st Highland Division and the 5th Division. They fought their way through Sicily and Italy until the German surrender on 2nd May 1945. Duties as forces of occupation followed until disbandment in November 1945.

The Lovat Scouts

Strictly speaking a Highland Regiment, nevertheless the Lovat Scouts maintained a close connection with Morayshire where it recruited and with Elgin where it maintained its Headquarters. Raised in the third month after the outbreak of the Boer War in 1899 it also served with distinction throughout both World Wars. One of the best-known Morayshire Men to serve in the Scouts was Capt. James Brander-Dunbar of Pitgaveny who saw service in all three wars. He served in the Sudan and in Africa during the Boer War, in France during the First World War and in the Home Guard during the Second World War when he commanded the Lossiemouth Platoon. Other well-known Morayshire men served during the Second World War in the Lovat Scouts including Lt Pelham Burn and Capt. Brodie of Brodie DSO. amongst others.

The Boer War ended in August 1902 and the Scouts came home and after a celebration at Beaufort Castle they were disbanded. Raised again as two mounted regiments of Yeomanry at the outbreak of the Second World War they were sent to garrison the Faroe Islands from 1940-1942 to deny them to German occupation. The regiment was frequently reorganised and re-equipped for different roles in 1942-3. As an infantry unit it was sent to Canada in 1944 for winter warfare training, including skiing. In July the regiment was sent to Italy where it chased the Germans north to Austria and then went to Greece until the war ended.

After hostilities ceased the regiment returned home and as on two previous occasions it was disbanded. Raised again in 1947, the Regiment continued to have a presence in Elgin until the mid 1980s when it was assumed into the 2nd 51st Highland Volunteers. The remnants of the Regiment are now based in Orkney and Shetland.

3 Division Training in Moray 1943 - 44

For the Invasion of Normandy (Operation 'Overlord' for land forces and Operation 'Neptune' for the Royal Navy), the Commander in Chief, General Eisenhower, Supreme Headquarters Allied Expeditionary Force (S.H.A.E.F.)

had 21st Army Group (Montgomery) with on the right the US 1st Army (Bradley), and on the left British 2nd Army (Dempsey). The US totalled twenty one divisions including one French; The British totalled eighteen divisions including one Polish; a grand total of thirty nine divisions.

21st Army group had under command on the right the 1st Canadian Army (Crerar) and on the left 2nd Army (Dempsey). 21st Army group had under command four corps, 1, 8, 12 and 30 and available for allocation to these corps the following divisions: Guards Armoured Division, 7th Armoured Division, 11th Armoured Division, 6th Airborne Division, 15th Scottish Division, 43rd Wessex Division, 49th West Riding Division, 50th Northumbrian Division, 53rd Welsh Division, 59th Staffordshire Division, 51st Highland Division and 3rd British Division, plus 4 Canadian Armoured Division, 2nd Canadian Division and 3rd Canadian Division and the 1st Polish Armoured Division. In addition to the foregoing, 21st Army Group had 79th Armoured Division comprising three armoured brigades, 30th, 1st Tank and 1st Assault Brigade RE plus various independent brigades and supporting units, Royal Artillery, Royal Signals, Royal Marines, Special Air Service etc.

3rd British Infantry Division

The 3rd British Infantry Division (to give it its full title and to differentiate from the 3rd Canadian Infantry Division) was commanded by Major General Tom Rennie, formerly of the Black Watch, 51st Highland Division and El-Alamein - where he won his DSO. The Division moved to Inverness/Moray area in December 1943. Divisional planning for Operation 'Overlord', the invasion of Europe, began at Aberlour House on 26 February 1943 and the Division met up with the Naval Task Force 'S', commanded by Rear-Admiral A.G.Talbot. Together with the Royal Navy, the Division perfected its landing techniques and between December 1943 and March 1944 made seven full-scale sea-borne landings on Moray Firth beaches. The last of the huge exercises, before the troops moved south, was on 17/18 March 1943 from Chanonry (Fort George) to sail north-east up the Moray Firth to Lybster and Wick. Despite very rough weather the 'attack' on Burghead was successful as the flotillas of LCTs landed under gunfire and RAF Sunderland's bombing cover. (Delaforce.1995:11).

It is interesting to remember that, almost exactly 900 years before, Burghead Bay saw the longships of Thorfinn the Mighty sailing down from Orkney to support his brother-in-law MacBeth at the battle of Torfness. Now the grey shapes of Royal Navy ships stealing into the beaches at dawn were rehearsing for the biggest invasion ever seen, one which comprised almost 6,500 ships. The forces employed in Overlord consisted of 2,878,439 Officers and men, plus a total of 9,901 aircraft of all types.

3 British Division, with which we are particularly concerned, comprised four brigades: 27th Armoured Brigade with 13th/18th Royal Hussars, 1st East Riding Yeomanry and Staffordshire Yeomanry; 9th Infantry Brigade comprising 1st Battalion Lincolns, 1st Battalion KOSB, 2nd Battalion Royal Ulster Rifles; 185 Brigade comprising 2nd Battalion Royal Warwicks, 1st Battalion Royal Norfolks, 2nd Battalion KSLI; 8th Brigade comprising 1st Battalion Suffolk, 2nd Battalion East Yorks and 1st Battalion South Lancs.

Strategy

General Montgomery records (Montgomery.1958:260). that his strategy was to maintain so much pressure on the Germans that they would commit their Panzers against 2nd British Army front on the left to ease the planned clearance of the Contentin Peninsula by the Americans and the capture of Cherbourg by US First Army. This port was critical for the logistic build up of the two allied armies.

The Division was tasked to be the left flank assault division of 21st Army Group landing between Lion-sur-Mer and Ouistreham. The immediate task was to secure the high ground north of Caen and if possible Caen itself, also to relieve the troops holding the bridges of the Caen Canal and the River Orne which had been seized during the preceding night by paratroops. In addition to the armour, the assault troops were 8 Brigade with 3 English County Regiments followed by 185 and then 9 Brigade, along with 1st Special Service Brigade and 4th Royal Marine Commando. In fact, leading elements of infantry did reach to within 3 miles of Caen on D-day but were insufficient in strength to take it - or to hold it even if they had been able to take it, but the high ground was secured.

All units of 21st Army Group were supported by units of 79th Armoured Division which was the parent division for specialised armour of "The Funnies" as they were called. These comprised:

- DCL which was a searchlight mounted on a tank.
- DD which was a Sherman tank adapted to swim.
- Crab which was a flail on the front of a Sherman gun tank.
- AVRE which was a Churchill tank adapted to carry various equipments and armed with a Petard and Besa.
- Crocodiles which were Churchill tanks towing armoured fuel trailers and having the ability to act as very effective flame throwers.

Moray and the Field of Battle

The beach obstacles facing the assault were - starting at low water - element C which was a sort of steel gate, metal stakes and mines, wooden knife rests and mines, tetrahedron and hedgehogs also with mines, wire entanglements, esplanades and sea walls, dunes, cliffs and anti-tank ditches and strong points with wire and mines. Some of the bunkers had concrete up to 10 feet thick.

The coast of Moray bore a remarkable similarity to the ground in Normandy over which the Division was destined to fight. Imagine yourself at the sea off Findhorn estuary (see Appendix 5). On your left lies Burghead, approximating to Ouistreham, whilst Newton tower lies near where Caen would be. On your right you see Nairn beach and Nairn town approximating to Arromanches, with further right Ardersier where the US 1st Army beaches lay.

On the British front Ouistreham (Burghead) to Arromanches (Nairn) was the zone allocated to the British 2nd Army which was to be assaulted by three Divisions with, on the right, the 50th Northumbrian Division, Sector Arromanches (Nairn) to Courseulles (Findhorn), 3 Canadian Division Sector Courselles (Findhorn) to Ouistreham (Burghead). That is the broad picture.

In addition there were various other Independent Brigades, Commando and Special Service Brigades etc. assaulting the same front with specific targets - e.g. coast-defence gun sites and other critical strong points, such as Radar and Command Centres. On our extreme left again, beyond Ouistreham over the canal and River Orne, the 6th Airborne Division (5 and 3 Para Brigades) were to capture bridges over the canal and river and establish a beachhead to facilitate a breakout eastwards in due course.

The Objective and 3rd British Division

Returning to 3 British Division assaulting with three Infantry Brigades, 8 Brigade followed by 185 Brigade and 9 Brigade. The 8 Brigade was supported by two squadrons Assault RE (AVRE's) and one squadron 22nd Dragoons with flail equipped tanks. Their primary objective was to form gaps through the defences to allow the follow up troops tanks, infantry and artillery etc. to pass through and secure a bridgehead.

This operation of landing on a strongly fortified coast had never yet been attempted in an area where the enemy expected attack and where for three years he had been preparing his defences with resources, ingenuity and using slave labour.

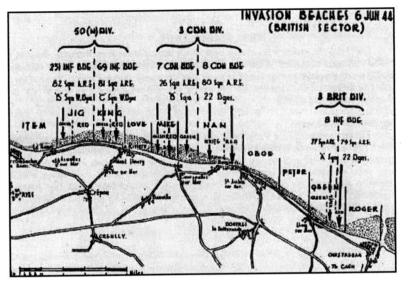

Fig 10. The British Sector for ' Overlord '
Courtesy The Tank Museum Bovington

Practice training in Moray

At selected areas training for Overlord began during the winter of 1943/44. Army, Corps and Divisional Planning Staff began work in January 1944. Final allocation of units to the order of battle for the assault started in March 1944. Some 3 British Divisional Planning was undertaken at Aberlour House, Aberlour and assault teams practised their role and techniques on the beaches of Moray.

At Aberlour stereoscopic air photographs from the saturation air sorties being flown daily by RAF over the invasion beaches and as a distraction over the Pas de Calais, showed the build up of German defences on the beaches to be captured. As each new type of obstacle was identified and located a decision was taken about how it was to be overcome. One of the 79th Armoured Division's 'funnies' would be selected and then the Landing Craft that was planned to land on that part of the beach had its loading table altered if necessary to ensure that the right equipment discharged onto the beach in the required order. As photos from each sortie were evaluated so the ships loading tables and the allocation of equipment was altered as necessary.

For exercises, Tank Landing craft would come into the beach below the walls of Fort George by Chanonry Narrows and the tanks would load into the ships. The flotilla then put to sea and sailed out into the Moray Firth until the following dawn when they found themselves in company with other ships, containing infantry brigades and supporting arms, approaching the beaches at Burghead Bay and Culbin Sands.

The landing beaches in France were heavily obstructed by a wide variety of obstacles and covered by fire. The Germans had three years of preparation, with General Rommel ultimately in charge, and huge quantities of slave labour. 'Monty' appointed Major-General Hobart of 79th Armoured Division to devise means of dealing with these obstacles. This was accomplished by using tanks fitted with various devices and crewed by assault troops including 5 Assault Regiment Royal Engineers, and in addition there were tanks equipped to clear mines and crewed by 22nd Dragoons as well as amphibious swimming tanks (DD tanks) crewed by 13th/18th Hussars. The armour cleared the obstacles and opened gaps in the defences and then with, their normal armament supported the infantry on to their objectives.

Needless to say there were unfortunate accidents including some fatalities incurred during these exercises, which to have any real value were conducted, as far as possible, under realistic conditions including the use of live ammunition and ordnance. There was a Battle School at Dunphail House where live ammunition was also used. It is reported that the DD tanks, which were vulnerable to swamping as well as to gear failure and enemy attention, lost at least one of their complement and that it still lies on the seabed in the vicinity of Burghead pier. The crews of these tanks were all issued with personal sets of Davis Escape apparatus as supplied to submariners for emergency use. There is also at least one DUKW on the bottom in Burghead Bay.

There is a further report of a macabre accident that befell the unfortunate crew of a Churchill tank. The winter of 1943-44 was very wet and cold and the ground in the exercise areas was soggy in parts. This crew, having successfully come ashore and achieved its objective was ordered to harbour up for the night. The custom was to position the tanks alongside buildings where their outline might merge into the building mass, with the use of camouflage netting, when seen from the air. This doomed tank snuggled up to the wall of Burgie School and the crew, as it was a very wet and cold night bivouacked under the tank, a usual procedure up until then. Sadly the tank settled down in the soft ground and killed its crew. A stern warning was immediately issued that in future tank crews would not take shelter under tanks, instead they rigged up a canvas cover from the side of the tank as a bivouac. In the interests of security and morale none of these sort of unfortunate and, in the circumstances, inevitable misfortunes ever received any publicity at the time and it has proved impossible to confirm these reports in the record today.

On D-day the assault was covered by a naval bombardment from *Warspite*, *Repulse*, and *Ramilles* and many other warships. Close support, however, was supplied by special ships each armed with 200 rocket-propelled mortars and these ships used live ammunition in training. Some of the live mortar rounds from these support ship bombardments were still being found from time to time in the Culbin Forest area for years after the war.

Local public involvement

The area westward from Netherton on the Findhorn estuary to Maviston Farm was cleared of all civilians in October 1943 at three week's notice by Admiralty order. Italian POW's, from camp 67 at Sandyhillock, Craigellachie, helped the farmers to lift potatoes from the clamps, cattle were sold, furniture was stored and all the people were evacuated. The area remained closed and deserted whilst the training with live ammunition was going on, but the people were eventually allowed back on to their farms and properties in May 1944. It is understood that compensation was promptly paid by the Admiralty and the principal loss sustained by the proprietors was that of their sink plugs. If you have ever tried to wash in a sink without a plug you will know why.

Summary

In the Battle of the Beaches the predominant and perhaps the decisive factor was the bold employment of specialised armour. On every beach where it was employed the assault went essentially as planned, in spite of the grave difficulties occasioned by the rough seas. Success could only have been achieved by the most careful organisation, training and rehearsal, the skilful co-ordination of all those services and the perfection of original techniques. Tactically, the great novelty was the surprise achieved by landing, in the first wave of invasion, a weight of armour great enough to overwhelm the defences in the first few hours. This was achieved by assigning to lead the attack on each beach both DD tanks and other specialised armour of 79th Armour Division. Where massed armour led with specialised tanks in the van, the hard crust was broken with a minimum loss of life and time.

In the planning stages the assaulting American troops, to the west, were offered the support of our specialised armour but the offer was declined with disastrous results on some of their more difficult beaches.

Eisenhower said in retrospect:

"Apart from the factor of tactical surprise the comparatively light casualties we sustained were in large measure due to the success of the novel mechanical contrivances we employed and the staggering moral

and material effect of the mass of armour landing in the leading waves of the assault. It is doubtful if the assault forces could have firmly established themselves without the assistance of these weapons. The first phase of the invasion, that is the opposed landing and formation of a secure bridge head, was critical to the success of the re-conquest of Europe."

The part played by this area in the training of these assault troops in the winter of 1943/44 is Moray's great contribution to the successful start of the second front and the eventual defeat of the Nazi War Machine.

In conclusion, a quote from Milton:

"Swift as the lightening glance he executes his errand on the wicked, who surprised, lose their defence, distracted and amazed."

The Home Guard

Introduction

When Britain had been seriously threatened by invasion during the Napoleonic Wars; a citizens' army of volunteers was formed and was immediately the focus of derision. As Orcadian Samuel Laing noted:

"Under the alarm of invasion every village, every street, set on foot its corps of volunteers. Drilling was the daily occupation of those whose previous habits of living were not the most adapted to the soldier's trade. Farce or caricature could represent nothing more ridiculous than the scene when sober, elderly, corpulent men, apothecaries, shopkeepers, and other respectable householders of the village were in all earnestness learning to march and to shoulder arms. The cheesemonger or draper, shouldering his firelock, the tailor marching with pointed toe, the grocer showing how fields were won were, no doubt, as individuals, ridiculous enough; their appearance under arms might not satisfy the soldier's eye, but it gave a new turn to the character of the nation when every respectable man was anxiously learning the duties of the private soldier."

One Hundred and forty years later, Britain was once again threatened with invasion and 14,300,000 leaflets were printed, 'If the Invader Comes' (see Appendix 1) with the stark message, 'The Germans threaten to invade Great Britain. Think before you act. But think always of your country before you think of yourself.' Eden spelled it out 'Now is your opportunity. We want large numbers of such men in Great Britain, who are British subjects, between the ages of seventeen and sixty five, to come forward now and offer their service in order to make assurance doubly sure. The name of the new force, which is now to be raised will be the 'Local Defence Volunteers'. This name describes its duties in three words. It must be understood that this is, so to speak, a spare time job so there is no need for any volunteer to abandon his present occupation.' On 16 May the BBC put out a general warning against parachutists and on the following day guards were posted at Broadcasting House and at most of the ministries in Whitehall.

Within five minutes of Eden's wireless announcement the first volunteer telephoned to the police station at Elgin, while the next to come forward was a retired Army captain who had served in the previous war. At Alves the village constable had not heard the broadcast announcement and was reluctant to take any action as the local farm workers arrived by foot and on bicycle to enlist. Eventually he produced a penny notebook and wrote down the names of the volunteers. Nobody knew what to do with the list of names. The instructions were to hand them to 'a properly appointed commander', but no such commander existed nor was there any arrangement for appointing one. Eventually the Lord Lieutenant in consultation with the military commander of the area selected a commander. The authorised establishment for Moray was 350, but when over 1,000 men volunteered the War Office increased the quota to that figure. Later, some 2,000 men were enlisted in the force. Nationwide, more than a quarter of a million men had volunteered in the first six days and by the 1st August the total had risen to more than a million. The difficulties attendant on the enrolment of such large numbers, with no organisation, no uniforms and no arms, were formidable.

The 18th Earl of Moray, Francis Douglas Stuart, M.C., accepted command of the volunteers who were initially formed into three platoons. The East (Lossiemouth) platoon was commanded by Captain J.Brander-Dunbar. The Central (Elgin) by Lt.Col. W.D.Allan, while the West (Forres) was placed in charge of Lt.Col. J.O. Hopkinson. All these officers had given distinguished service in the First World War, but except for the Bonny Earl, they were all of an age when the sobriquet 'dug-out' could be properly applied.

James Brander-Dunbar was born at Pitgaveny on the 10th October 1875 and he was almost forty when he enlisted in the Cameron Highlanders on the 4th of August 1914. Twice wounded in action he was aged 64 when he took over command of the Lossiemouth platoon. He kept a diary of these momentous days and the trenchant comments of this gifted and energetic officer are illuminating indeed. After the codeword Cromwell had been issued in

September 1940 the 2i/c of one of the Home Guard sections refused to turn out and Pitgaveny noted 'I don't imagine it was funk so much as d----d laziness'.

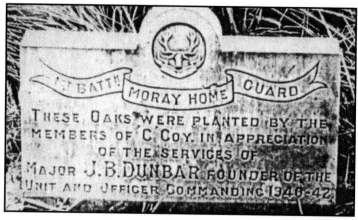

Fig 11. A stone beside five oak trees planted in front of Pitgaveny house. It reads - '1st Battn. MORAY HOME GUARD These oaks were planted by the members of C Coy. in appreciation of the services of Major J B DUNBAR founder of the Unit and Officer Commanding 1940-42'.
Courtesy of A.J. Dunbar

Lt.Col. W.D.Allan was not quite sixty when he responded to the call to arms. He had served in South Africa but his active service World War I experience had been cut short when he was invalided home after the battle of Mons in 1914. Lt.Col. J.O. Hopkinson was born at Willesden, Middlesex on May 19th, 1877, so he was sixty three when once more he put on his uniform with the African General Service medal; The Somaliland 1902-04 with clasps; Pip, Squeak and Wilfred from W.W.I; the M.C.; D.S.O. and bar; Crois de Chevalier of the Legion of Honour and the Croix de Guerre.

The rank and file volunteers comprised mainly ex-soldiers and youngsters who were waiting their call-up. There was also a useful leavening of men who were just too young to have served in the First War and were now slipping into age groups unlikely to be called to front line military service in this new war. In Moray, a predominately rural county, there were also many young fit workers who were employed on farms and were, for the time being at least, in reserved occupations and therefore excused from conscription.

The three platoons were each divided into three sections. In the Eastern No. One Platoon No1 Section, commanded by Professor E.L.Collis, guarded Lossiemouth and Lhanbryde. No.2 Section, under A.Campbell, looked after Garmouth, Urquhart and Mosstodloch while No.3, with R.J.Mackenzie in charge, had responsibility for Longmorn and Tiendland to the Spey. Under

Lt.Col. W.D.Allan's Central or No.Two Platoon, Captain S.I.Russell was in charge of No.1 Section which covered Hopeman, Burghead and Spynie. No. 2 Section was commanded by Sgt.W.Proctor, D.C.M., M.M. and its district extended from the south side of Elgin High Street to Dallas, Kellas, Pluscarden and Birnie. No 3 Section, under Cpt. G.A.Greig, looked after the rural areas of Dallas, Kellas, Birnie and Pluscarden.

The Western No.Three Platoon, with its headquarters at Forres, had its No.1 Section under Major Falconer, D.S.O.,M.C., and control of Forres, Findhorn, Darnaway and Dyke while No.2 Section, Major the Hon.R.Bruce in command, looked after the estates of Dunphail and Altyre. No.3 Section, operated independently under Capt.F.C. Hendry, O.B.E., and was responsible for Grantown, Cromdale, Advie and Dava. In addition there were volunteer units formed by railway and post office workers.

Initially, the Local Defence Volunteers had neither uniforms nor weapons and, at this stage, neither rank nor badges of rank. All were volunteers, but as can be seen from the initial organisation, some were more equal than others. Volunteers were issued with red flannel armbands with the black letters L.D.V. stencilled on. The production of these armbands was carried out, under conditions of theatrical secrecy, at Elgin Academy. Later, these were replaced by centrally issued khaki brassards. There were no regular weapons, but in a substantially rural community there were plenty of shotguns and more than a few .22 and larger calibre rifles. The police turned a blind eye when unlicensed souvenirs were handed in for issue to the volunteers. A shotgun is a devastating weapon at short range but hopeless at ranges beyond 30m (100ft). However, by pouring melted wax into the cartridges the lead pellets could be fired as a solid lump which would make a horrible hole in a door, or man, at 100m (110 yds).

During rhe summer of 1940 the volunteers drilled and guarded bridges and beaches. They checked the newly issued identity cards and while they intercepted no fifth columnists nor enemy paratroopers disguised as nuns, by their ubiquitous presence they curtailed the activities of the poaching fraternity. Although it has to be admitted that some members of the force were not above helping the odd salmon to grass itself.

The log book of 'A' company, 4 Platoon of Moray LDV has survived and every night some four to six volunteers gathered at York Tower, Newton from 9.30 in the evening to 5.30 next morning to watch and wait for an enemy who never came. There was a column for Patrol Leaders' Remarks and this was regularly empty until the 30th August when an exasperated Alan Rose wrote 'What about the explosions between 11.07 and 12 pm' and next day he again commented, 'Did no one hear the bombs about 11.00p.m' Regrettable though it may be one is left with the suspicion that the guardsmen were not as alert as they should have been. Perhaps harsh words were exchanged for the following night the 1st September at 10.45pm it was noted, 'Flashes of gun-fire and loud reports heard towards the North.West. Great aeroplane activity also observed. A light observed at one of the windows of Newton House.'

On the 4th September at 10 pm, 'Aeroplane crashed south-east of Strath Mayne. Reflection of fire in the clouds still to be seen at 11pm' The night of 7th September was noted as, 'night of General Alarm' when 25 guardsmen were present from 9.30pm to 8am and, it was further noted that the six who would normally be on duty, i.e. Messrs David M.Leitch, Robert Gardiner, James Smith, Alan McRae and James Allan were paid 3/- (15p) each.

Once everybody had been issued with L.D.V. (widely believed to stand for 'look, duck and vanish') brassards, Winston Churchill, in a memorable broadcast on 14th July proposed that the name of the volunteer force be changed to 'Home Guard'. New brassards were distributed and on 8th August the first khaki denim uniforms were issued at Elgin. Somewhat earlier an issue was made of about 100 P14 rifles and this was followed by the issue of heavily greased P17 rifles.

The standard rifle ammunition during the First and Second wars was a .303 calibre, Mk.VII bullet fired from a rimmed cartridge. That is, the cartridge had a rim round its base and this rim was seized by the extraction mechanism after the round had been fired. Most other countries used rimless ammunition where there was a groove at the rear of the cartridge to allow of extraction. The rifle designed to take the rimmed ammunition was originally the Lee-Metford which was introduced in 1889 and modified into the Lee-Enfield in 1900. After the Boer War the rifle was further modified and was designated the S.M.L.E. (the short model Lee-Enfield) and it was this weapon that was used during the whole of World War I and, after simplification, during World War II. It was not however used by the Home Guard.

The Home Guard was eventually issued with a rifle with a .300 calibre bullet fired from a rimless cartridge. Thus the luckless Home Guard could not use the ammunition, which was .303, fired from his machine gun or indeed could not use any of the standard ammunition issued to the regular troops. How this peculiar state of affairs came about is a long but interesting story.

During the Boer War the British troops were equipped with the Lee-Enfield which was a rifle where the locking lugs, which secured the mechanism at the moment of firing, were at the rear of the bolt. This meant that they could be easily cleaned and it also meant that the bolt action to remove a fired cartridge and place a new one in the breech was easily and quickly accomplished. There was just one drawback to the rifle. Because the whole of the bolt was under compression at the moment of firing the consequent accuracy was impaired. This was not important at close range, say under 300m, but above 600m the effect began to be noticeable.

The Boers were equipped with Mauser action rifles where the locking lugs were at the front of the bolt. Difficult of access for cleaning and with an awkward bolt action yet, with only a small section of the bolt under compression, their riflemen were able to pick off the British at ranges well beyond accurate fire from the S.M.L.E. After the war the British military decided to abandon the 303 Lee-Enfield and issue the troops with a new .276 calibre Mauser action rifle which was introduced in 1913 and hence was called the Pattern 13 or P13 for short. However, before the P13 could be issued to more than a few troops, war broke out in August 1914 and the decision was taken to retain the .303 calibre S.M.L.E. And fortunate it was that the British troops were equipped with the sweet and simple bolt action rifle which produced such rapid fire that at Mons the Germans believed that they were facing massed machine guns.

The P13 was re-chambered to take a .303 cartridge and was issued as a sniper's weapon., the P14. As all the factories in Britain were geared to producing the Lee-Enfield the patterns for the P14 were shipped to the U.S.A. and three companies manufactured them there. These were, Remington Arms Co., Remington Arms Union and the Winchester Repeating Arms co. When America entered the war in 1917 there was an immediate demand for the Springfield rifle, the standard issue weapon of the American army, but the three major manufacturers were already equipped to mass produce the P14 so, with a slight modification, the .303 P14 was re-chambered as the .300 rimless P17 and issued in lieu of the Springfield.

When the war ended in 1918 the surplus to requirements P17's were smothered in grease and put into storage and were then sold to the British in those desperate days of early 1940. And that is how the Home Guard in Moray, and elsewhere in these islands, came to be equipped with a weapon which had been designed for the war before the last and, crucially, used different ammunition to that of the regular army.

Fortunately these rifles were never fired in anger, though many thought that they would be used on the evening of the 7th September 1940. It had been a warm day with a harvest moon. All day the horse reapers had scythed the golden grain and the 'stooks' stood straight in the fields like guardsmen on parade. As the tired workers went to bed, telephones were ringing in isolated farms and in the towns and villages, men on bicycles called up at windows, 'It's on, this is it'. Shotguns and rifles were picked up while wives and mothers made up flasks and sandwiches. There were hasty farewells as the men went to their posts. The night was oppressive with a peculiar mixture of silence and rumour. Those who had rifles counted their pitifully small quantity of ammunition. Dawn brought the order 'Stand down' and everybody went home. Somebody had given the code word CROMWELL which immediately activated the overall defence of Great Britain, although it was actually only a stand-to order that had been misunderstood. Was it just a dress rehearsal? By the British or by the Germans? Few knew then, fewer know now.

Conventional weapons issued during 1940 to the Moray Home Guard comprised 40 light machine guns, 4 heavy Vickers machine guns, 95 Boys Anti-tank rifles, and 130 P17 rifles. The latter were soon reduced to 129, when a Home Guardsman at Lossiemouth allowed sand into his rifle and as he fired on the range the barrel of his gun split from foresight down to the breech A most serious and tragic accident occurred later in the war when a thirty year old Moray guardsman was accidentally shot dead by a colleague.

By 1942 another 440 P17's had been issued as well as 240 Sten guns, 34 spigot mortars and 60 Tommy guns. But as well as guns, the Guardsmen wanted ranks and on August 15th 1940 the Army Council issued an Instruction allowing the differentiation of ranks by means of broad dark blue stripes on shoulder straps, ranging from a Zone Commander with one broad stripe to Platoon Commander with one narrow stripe. This arrangement lasted until the 6th November 1940 when it was announced in the House of Commons that ranks similar to those held in the army, would be allowed in the Home Guard. However it was not until the 13th of March that officers were allowed to wear their badges of rank. This strange reluctance to allow Home Guard officers to wear badges of rank, comparable to those authorised by the regular army, surely indicates that, behind the scenes, Colonel Blimp was putting up fierce resistance to any dilution of the army's prestige.

By 1942 the Home Guard was not recognisable as the once eager but untrained Local Defence Volunteers. It was more like a cadet force, training people for the regular army and, where possible, taking over regular army duties. The old original dug-outs had been pensioned off. The existing commander, Col.J.O.Hopkinson, DSO, MC, retired at the age of 65 in July 1942 and was succeeded by Major J.N.Petrie who was promoted to Lt.-Col. and took over command of the Battalion. Conscription for the Guard had been introduced on 16th February 1942 and a battle school, though not under the aegis of the Moray command, was established at Humbreck Farm on the hillside just to the south of Millbuies. In January 1942 the War Office gave authority for the Home Guard to man AA and coastal batteries and by March 1943 the local gun emplacements were substantially manned by local part-time personnel.

Medical arrangements, at first very rudimentary, had originally been under the control of Professor E.L. Collis, a most distinguished physician who in turn was instructed by Col. A.D.Macdonald. Eventually First Aid Sections were organised on the basis of one section per platoon with stretcher bearers equipped with red cross brassards and Geneva Certificates. If required to take up arms the bearers were ordered to discard their brassards and certificates before firing their rifles.

By 1942 the basic but meagre petrol ration was abolished and only essential civilian users were issued with coupons. Unfortunately, the majority of Home Guard personnel were not eligible for petrol supplies and this considerably hampered their operations. However, with the introduction of conscription and the tacit acceptance that the Home Guard was really a somewhat exotic army unit, transport and fuel were supplied on an official basis. Most welcome was the issue of motor cycles and by 1943 the Moray Home Guard had eight motor cycles and the requisite Dispatch Riders to roar importantly about on them.

From April 1941 there was an Intelligence Section, but whether this liaised with or used the services of the Pigeon Service is not known. This latter service functioned for two years but was wound up in April 1943, allegedly due to the shortage of pigeon food. This seems like a doubtful allegation for in the Laich of Moray, with its multitude of farms, there must have been the opportunity to obtain enough gleanings to keep the pigeons fed. Certainly the Home Guard, substantially rural based, was used to help with the harvests and in the autumns of 1942, 43 and 44, the Government issued instructions to the Home Guard to reduce the number of exercises and parades and to encourage the men to work on the harvest.

No Scottish army unit considers itself complete unless it has a pipe band and by September 1943 the Moray Home Guard could parade and march behind its very own band. The uniforms were mostly on loan, mainly from the Territorial Army so the prevailing tartan was the Seaforth. By this time the Home Guard uniform had been standardised with the issue of serge battle dress. But there were subtle differences from the regular army. The belt and gaiters were leather instead of the usual webbing while the shoulder flash read Home Guard. The decisive difference however was in the rifle, which was the P17, using the .300 rimless cartridge.

With America now in the war, ammunition was no longer in short supply and the Home Guard rifle had one great advantage over the regular army; it had a formidable bayonet which, as Corporal Jones was always reminding the others in his unit 'they don't like it up em.' By this time the regular army had equipped its troops with a pathetic spike bayonet, looking like an 8" (13cm) nail, ignorant of the fact that the soldier rarely used his bayonet to stick anybody but used it to chop wood, lever open ammunition boxes, and open tins etc., all of which are best carried out with a blade.

In 1944 the Home Guard, albeit unintentionally, altered the map of Moray. In the early summer they were practising firing mortar shells and, in thick fog, directed a steady fire from Covesea towards the sea. When firing stopped they descended the cliffs to see where their bombs had landed and discovered that they had demolished the sandstone pillar known as The Gows' Castle.(NGR NJ 176709) However the name was then transferred to an adjacent structure and the name retained on the map. Gow is a local name for the seagull and the rocky stack was a favourite nesting site for these birds.(A.J. Dunbar. *Pers commn*).

Fig 12. The Gows' Castle
From a painting courtesy of G. Sutherland

As the war progressed in Europe, so the need for the Home Guard diminished and on 6th September 1944 the Home Guard moved from conscription back to a voluntary basis and on November 1st a further order was given to 'Stand down.' The final parade was organised for the 3rd December 1944 and commenced at 14.00 at Borough Briggs when Lt.Col.J.N.Petrie opened the ceremony by reading the Royal Proclamation.

The Rev.G.S.Peebles of Birnie, Padre to the Moray Home Guard, then conducted a short service which was followed by a march past through the High Street to the saluting base in the Cooper Park where Col.A.D.Macdonald, took the salute accompanied by many local dignitaries.

The Battalion Commander, Lt.Col. J.N.Petrie then addressed his troops for the last time, finishing with 'Gentlemen of the 1st Moray Battalion Home Guard, I salute you!'

Although the Home guard was never tested in action they were able to render valuable service helping to make good the numbers suddenly required to guard vulnerable points, essential works and offices, road blocks, bridges, water supplies and power plants and many others. In addition there was patrolling to guard against saboteurs and parachutists or enemy agents infiltrating the area.

Now, sixty years after the Home Guard stood down, one can dispassionately look at their effectiveness. There is no evidence that their presence in any way deterred Hitler from ordering the invasion of Britain. If the Germans had invaded Britain in 1940 the enthusiastic but ill-equipped volunteers would have been easy meat for the tough and battle experienced enemy.

Later, as the Home Guard became more professional it became more effective and performed valuable work, both in training men for the forces and releasing regular soldiers from static defence duties. Their arms became more effective. 240 Sten guns were issued in 1942, but it was a blessing that three men from the Home Guard, armed with a Smith gun, never had to face three Germans behind a PAK (anti-tank gun). The Smith gun deserves a chapter all to itself. Even then it is doubtful if justice could ever be done to the brave men who were prepared to handle such a clumsy, dangerous and utterly useless weapon.

Although Americans, estimated by *The Times* to number some 4,000, in Britain at the start of the war were advised on 17th May 1940 by the U S Embassy,. to return home without delay by way of Eire, some elected to stay. In early June the 1st American Squadron of the Home Guard was formed. It was commanded by General Wade H. Hayes and mustered some 60-70 who wore the British Home Guard uniform with the addition of a red eagle shoulder-flash. This was all strongly disapproved of by the U S Ambassador, Kennedy.

Notwithstanding the American contribution, The Home Guard was typically British. Initially voluntary, sometimes comic, occasionally chaotic, but the men were prepared to fight and die for what they believed in. Most of those who stepped forward to defend these shores over sixty years ago have now faded away and this chapter is a tribute to their devotion and to the memory of the 1,206 (Fleming.1957:207fn). members of the Home Guard who lost their lives as a result of wounds, injuries or illness due to their service.

A nominal roll of the Moray Home Guard Auxilliary Units is included at Appendix 3. In the absence of evidence the date of this roll must be assumed. Judging by the names and ranks it seems probable that it was an early roll at the time the units were being formed. Naturally some names and ranks changed during the war but it is interesting to note that later on nearly every section was commanded by an officer and that most of them were the headmasters of the local schools.

'The Women's home guard'

As the war ground on and men were called up for the regular forces, so women had slowly taken up positions once thought impossible or unsuitable for them. The Home Guard was to be no exception and on 15th April 1943 the War Office allowed women to join the Home Guard as Auxiliaries. Their position was formalised on 19th July 1943 when, following a War Office proclamation the Auxiliaries were known as 'The Women's Home Guard' and were issued with a plastic badge with the letters HG within a laurel wreath. They were not, however, supplied with a uniform until later, of these seventeen pioneering ladies in Moray who took advantage of the order are as follows:-

Mrs. J.Allan	Tel Op
Miss O.Anderson	Tel Op
Miss M.R. Brown	Clerkess
Miss G.Browse	Transport
Miss M.Browse	Transport
Mrs.A. Campbell	Clerkess
Mrs.E.L.Collis	Driver
Miss M.Davidson	Tel Op
Miss R.Ewen	Tel Op
Miss M.Farquhar	Transport
Miss A.Gault	Clerkess
Miss J.Harthill	Clerkess
Miss J.Leslie	Tel Op
Miss M.Scott	Tel Op
Miss E.I.Shepherd	Tel Op
Mrs.G.Simpson	Caterer
Miss G.Wilson	Typist

Fig 13. Gladys Browse
and May Farquhar
Note the headlamp blackout mask
Photo: Courtesy Mrs G. Smith.

The British Resistance

Introduction

During the early years of World War Two Britain was the only country in Europe to have a resistance recruited, armed and trained to fight in the event of invasion by enemy forces. When the survivors of the British Expeditionary Force had been evacuated from Dunkirk, after the fall of France, Britain stood alone and virtually defenceless.

A broadcast appeal on 15 May for men to form a Local Volunteer Defence force received an overwhelming response. Arms were scarce; most of the BEF equipment having been deliberately rendered useless and left behind in France, but they were supplemented from private sources by shotguns, sporting rifles and anything else that could conceivably be used as a weapon. On 4 June Winston Churchill prepared the nation for invasion saying 'We shall defend our island whatever the cost may be. We shall fight on the beaches, we shall fight on the landing grounds, we shall fight in the fields and in the streets, we shall fight in the hills, we shall never surrender'.

On 18 June Churchill made another famous broadcast to the country when he said:

> "The Battle of France is over. The Battle of Britain is about to begin. The whole fury and might of the enemy must soon be turned against us. Hitler knows he will have to break us in this island or lose the war. Let us therefore brace ourselves to our duty and so bear ourselves that if the British Empire and its commonwealth lasts for a thousand years men will still say - this was their finest hour."

On 23 July the LDV was renamed 'The Home Guard'. In the air the RAF was involved in a life or death struggle with the Luftwaffe attempting to win supremacy in the air prior to the German invasion codenamed SEALION. On 7 September a massive enemy raid on London signalled the start of the 'Blitz'. Failure of the Luftwaffe to gain control of the air turned Hitler's attention from 'Sealion' to the invasion of Russia called operation BARBAROSSA. In Britain the immediate threat of invasion was lessened but by no means dispelled.

Auxiliary Units

The idea of forming a stay-behind guerrilla force has been credited to Captain Peter Fleming, elder brother of Ian Fleming, of James Bond fame, who was serving in XII Corps under General Andrew Thorn, Grenadier Guards who was persuaded to set up covert observation units. These units were later to form the nucleus of the Auxiliary Units of the Home Guard. The title Auxiliary Units was deliberately chosen as being sufficiently innocuous as to arouse no special interest in its cover role. The Auxiliary Units were formed in conditions of great secrecy. All personnel were required to sign the official Secrets Act. Peter Wilkinson (later Sir Peter Wilkinson KC, MO, DSO, OBE) who was later to join the SOE, was at that time a serving officer in the Royal Fusiliers and was given the job, along with Colonel Colin Gubbins, of organising these new units for which he wrote an instruction manual that was disguised as a Diary.

Auxiliary units eventually came under command of Col. Gubbins, GHQ Staff Home Forces. During July 1940 the Auxiliary Units were being formed with patrols of sometimes up to a maximum of 14 men but more usually 8 men including a patrol leader, usually a sergeant. Each group of four patrols, or sections, was under command of a group leader generally designated an Intelligence Officer. These I.Os were tasked with recruiting and forming the units, distributing stores, training and acting as liaison with military commanders as required. For security reasons in case of capture, interrogation and torture there was no contact with other patrols and only the patrol leader knew the group leader. Formed of men with an intimate knowledge of their own areas they dropped out of their ordinary Home Guard units and trained to go underground when the invasion came.

The highly covert character of this organisation meant that no records were kept but it is estimated that about 3,500 men were recruited and embodied in three separate battalions nos. 201,202, and 203 in 14 areas from Wick to Sussex. With his well known enthusiasm for irregular forces the idea was encouraged by Winston Churchill, one of the very few people who were aware of the existence of this secret army. In his memo to the Secretary of State for War 25-08-40 he says:

> *"I have been following with much interest the growth and development of the new guerrilla formations of the home Guard known as Auxiliary Units... From what I hear these units are being organised with thoroughness and imagination and should, in the event of invasion, prove a useful addition to the regular forces. Perhaps you will keep me informed of progress."* (Churchill.1949. 584)

Formed to harass the enemy if Britain was to be over-run they would go to ground in secret bunkers or OB's (operating bases), built in conditions of total secrecy by Royal Engineers or civilian contractors, sworn to secrecy, in out of the way places and woodlands with heavily camouflaged entrances and exits. The bunkers could accommodate a section for up to 14 days. Secretly and carefully recruited the men were sometimes subject to positive vetting by army Field Security Police with links back to Scotland Yard and MI 5. Not everybody approached for recruitment was in favour of the Auxiliary Units having a real and logical concern about the inevitable reprisals that their activities would undoubtedly attract. Although it is known to have occurred elsewhere there is no record of any such view having been expressed locally.

To preserve their anonymity these men were not on official army lists but were borne on the strength of Home Guard battalion HQs for records and allowances. The Home Guard was used as a cover and the men were covertly embodied. With the probability that they would operate mostly under cover of darkness an intimate knowledge of their own areas was essential. Recruitment was mainly amongst farmers, gamekeepers, foresters, estate workers etc. Locally many schoolmasters were recruited and in most cases were commissioned as patrol leaders. Group leaders were usually from the regular army as were the training staffs. Local units, part of 201 Battalion, came under the command of Major Reginald Gordon-Lennox (Scot's Guards), with HQ at Blairmore house near Huntly, who had a training staff of regular soldiers.

Fig 14. Blairmore House
Photo: W A B

Weapons

After Dunkirk when most of the equipment of the BEF had to be destroyed and abandoned on the beaches. Weapons of all descriptions were in very short supply in 1940 despite the ship loads being sent with all haste from America.

Winston Churchill's son-in-law, Captain Duncan Sandys who was later appointed Depute Minister of Supply, now enters the picture with a memo of 8 August 1940, which he sent to Winston Churchill reporting on the progress being made in the Auxiliary Units and asking, in effect, for their fair share in the allocation of weapons to them. This resulted in the supply of rifles and bayonets, Mills grenades, delay action time pencil fuses, pressure release and pull switches, plastic high explosive, gun cotton slabs and primers and various types of incendiary bombs.

A future supply of Tommy guns together with reserves of food and water was also noted. By early 1940 Smith and Wesson 0.38 revolvers had also been issued at Churchill's insistence together with 0.22 rifles with telescopic sights and silencers and commando knives.(the rifle was thought to be useful for shooting guard dogs etc. and with a high velocity bullet could kill a man at long range). The first issue of Sten guns was also made but it was never a popular weapon for covert work, being too noisy and difficult to control the rate of fire between one round and the whole magazine.

There seems to have been a variety in the type of weapons supplied, presumably depending on availability and maybe in some cases on special requirements, For instance, some sections were supplied with brass knuckle dusters and sniper rifles and in one case with an automatic Browning repeating rifle. Detonators and fast and slow cordite fuses were also issued, some sections had a Bren gun, others had a Lewis gun.

The Darnaway Section had an inflatable dinghy to be used for crossing over the River Findhorn as their primary role was the destruction of any enemy aircraft, which might have taken over the Brackla Airfield or any enemy activity in the Mundole, Waterside, Balnageith areas or at Kinloss airfield. Tinned food and water stocks seem to have ranged from 2 to 6 weeks. Some sections had self-heating tins of soup. The men were also encouraged to live off the land as far as possible, no doubt the gamekeepers were to the fore in this activity. Some sections had rubber truncheons and there was also a jar of Navy issue rum for emergency use.

Uniforms

The issue of regular serge battledress and greatcoats quickly replaced the original issue of denim overalls. Rubber soled boots were issued along with the standard mixture of leather and webbing Home Guard equipment together with steel helmets and forage caps. At a later date the forage caps were replaced by balmorals all wearing the Seaforth Highlanders cap badge. Gas masks and camouflage creams were issued. Although Home Guard shoulder titles were worn the distinguishing letters and numerals identifying Home Guard battalions were not worn in order to preserve anonymity and avoid awkward questions about their supposed membership of the battalion.

Regular Home Guard units in Scotland and Northumberland were part of 201 (GHQ Reserve) Battalion and wore the numerals on both sleeves below the shoulder flash. Units were also supplied with field dressings and first aid equipment including morphia, blankets, ground sheet, water bottle, and gad capes and gloves, face veil and mess tin with knife, fork and spoon.

Operating Bases

The operating bases, OB's, or underground bunkers. were constructed clandestinely and were generally about ten feet underground and often dug into a bank or rising ground. They were large enough to accommodate each section, lined and roofed with corrugated iron supported by logs and they were entered by a camouflaged manhole giving access to a shaft with a ladder or rungs. At the foot of the shaft was a well and sill to contain the blast if a grenade was dropped down the shaft.

The main chamber had full standing headroom and was provided with space for the stores of food and water. Tiered wooden bunks were provided with wire frames; Ventilation shafts were constructed and camouflaged and there was an emergency exit with a chemical closet in an alcove Candles, hurricane and tilly lamp, primus stove and kettle, pots and pans and paraffin and petrol together with a spade, pick, axe and auger completed the basic equipment. Patrols were always most careful when approaching and leaving the hideaway to vary their routes to avoid creating a recognisable track and leaving any traces. Track discipline was scrupulously observed, as was the disposal of rubbish.

Adjacent to and in touch with the OB by telephone a two-man OP (observation post) was sometimes constructed in the vicinity of the main traffic routes. One of the duties of Auxiliary Units was to gather intelligence about enemy dispositions and troop movements from behind enemy lines for the use of home forces. The main function, however, was to act offensively in the rear of enemy troops particularly tanks and soft transport, small enemy posts and stragglers. Their activities would also include sniping and disrupting road and rail transport by sabotage and ambushes. In this area the principal targets would have been enemy aircraft on the many local airfields.

Each section had its HQ in the area where stores were kept. These included their explosives and devices such as booby traps and training stores together with a stock of piano wire for use to ambush motor cycle patrols. These stores were usually located in garden sheds, outhouses, stable blocks, garages etc., attached to country houses sufficiently far away from the OB. for there to be no obvious connection.

Parades, Training and Exercises

Parades were held weekly and training was carried out, the use of grenades and explosives was practised in old quarries whilst small arms training was carried out on rifle ranges arranged for the purpose in covert locations. Weekends were usually devoted to exercises when the OB might be occupied and a dummy attack launched against home forces targets. The radar post at Damhead near Kinloss, for example, was used as a target by the Spynie section while Brackla airfield was used as a target by the Darnaway section.

The Auxiliary Units had a secret training school at Coleshill House, Highworth near Swindon in Wiltshire to which units were sent for intensive training. Here courses were held with daytime lectures and demonstrations and exercises at night. In order to avoid compromising each other patrols from some distance apart would attend together. The regular army provided the training staff, unarmed combat was taught and practised. Methods of silent killing were demonstrated and learned together with field craft and booby trap assembly and deployment.

Training was based on the assumption that if captured the Auxiliary unit members would be shot out of hand. An order drafted by the German Army Commander-in-Chief, General Walter Von Brauchitsch, which was to have been posted as a decree in occupied Britain, stated, 'I warn all civilians that if they undertake active operations against the German forces they will be condemned to death inexorably'. Patrol members were prepared to accept death at the hands of their own comrades if necessary, rather than to fall into the hands of the enemy and under interrogation and torture risk compromising the movement. Today this sounds an extreme measure but must be taken in the context of the conditions which could have existed in occupied Britain when the activities of the Auxiliary Units would have been very much a last ditch effort.

Communications

As already mentioned patrols and sections worked independently of each other clandestinely and in isolation for security reasons and so that one could not compromise another. Thus lateral communication between units was non-existent unless established accidentally. Units communicated back to their Commands by runner or telephone and Commands forward to HQ in a similar manner.

Existing in tandem with the guerrilla sections of Auxiliary Units there was a covert communications radio network. Neither of these organisations had any knowledge that the other existed. The net was designated Auxiliary Unit Signals Home Forces and was recruited in much the same covert manner as the guerrilla units. Manned by a small proportion of Royal Signals personnel the bulk of the members came from the ATS (Auxiliary Territorial Service), VAD (Volunteer Aid Detachment) or FANYs (First Aid Nursing Yeomanry), although there were also civilians employed. The units came under command GHQ Auxiliary Units Signals.

Beatrice Temple, the Adjutant ATS, for whom the recruits undertook a voice test, selected the women for their clear and authoritative voices. They were required to sign the Official Secrete Act and attended a course at Coleshill House where they were instructed in unarmed combat, weapons training and the use of voice only transceivers. On posting they occupied hidden radio bases in clandestine locations.

Each base or out-station, of which there were hundreds countrywide, sometimes located in country houses or shacks in wooded areas, had its own underground zero station to which the operators would retire if the invasion occurred. They were called zero stations because when broadcasting from them the station code name was used with the suffix 'O'. These underground bases were smaller than the OB's of the guerrilla units having only accommodation for three operators but with bunks, weapons, food stocks etc., as required. Concealed entrances and exits were contrived as for the OB's. Each station had its own group of civilian runners who would take and collect messages from secret dead letter boxes.

Adjacent houses were often used as billets for Royal Signals personnel who serviced the radios. Out-stations were linked to control stations and they in turn were linked by telephone to GHQ Home Forces. Beatrice Temple recalled 32 of these controls, one of which was located in Elgin, another in Aberdeen. There is a persistent rumour that 'Rotha House' in Reidhaven Street Elgin was used as a clandestine base. Unfortunately the building has been so altered over the years that today it is not possible to identify where a hidden compartment might have been contrived. The building was variously used as an army billet or a Home Guard HQ during the war but it is of a size and design where a base could easily have been concealed whilst its role as a billet or HQ would have provided cover. Regretably it has proved impossible to discover any of the operators who may have been employed in the local communications network.

Whereas London and the industrial Midlands of England were considered as Hitler's prime targets in the event of invasion and defence lines were hastily constructed on this appreciation, the lines were continued up the east coast to include the Firth of Forth as the likeliest approach to Edinburgh, a prestigious target second only to London, perhaps. Morayshire was an obvious and very likely target area with its airfields at Balnageith, Kinloss, Lossiemouth, Bogs of Mayne, Dallachy, Brackla and Milltown. The capture of any one of these would have put the whole of Scotland within bomber range. The extensive beaches offered ideal sites for sea-borne assault and indeed the beach between Burghead and the Old Bar to the west of Findhorn was actually used during the winter of 1943 by the Third British Division to practise their forthcoming part in operation 'OVERLORD,' the invasion of Normandy as described elsewhere.

Beach defences included barbed wire and mines, anti-tank ditches and concrete blocks defended by pillboxes and with anti-air-landing poles in open areas. A coastal battery was sited at the Boar's Head between Lossiemouth and Kingston. All this was the special responsibility of regular forces and to a later extent of the Home guard but in the event it was over-run it would fall to the Auxiliary Units as a last ditch responsibility to wage guerrilla warfare in the enemy's rear. As the Auxiliary Units were a top-secret organisation documentation was severely limited and of that little remains available for research but copies of Peter Wilkinson's training manual, already mentioned, disguised as a diary exist along with Auxiliary Unit Signals passes.

With the passing years, unfortunately most of the men who served in the Auxiliary Units are now deceased. Some of the few remaining have been helpful with their recollections in building up a picture of the units in Morayshire and district. (see Appendix 3) Although for security reasons sections were supposed to operate in isolation this did not always happen and some sections combined with their neighbours for training and exercises against regular forces. Spynie and Burgie sections combined for operations against the RAF at Damhead near Kinloss, as has already been mentioned.

The only sections positively identified are those at Spynie, Burgie, Darnaway, Keith and Huntly at Gartly. Other sections mentioned by survivors but not corroborated include Lethen NGR NJ9351, Drummuir NGR NJ 3844. and Dufftown NGR NJ 3240. Spynie OB was in the woods at Aldroughty beside the A96 at NGR NJ 175628. The section HQ was in the coach house at Ardgilzean and this is where they kept their stores. There was also an OB, possibly manned by a section from Lhanbryde, in the vicinity of 'Cascade' on the Orton Road near NGR NJ 278595 The Darnaway section had its OB near Berrylea Farm on the bank of the River Findhorn at NGR NJ 008585. This was later moved to a new site at NGR NJ 005562. The section HQ was at Darnaway Castle. There was a section stationed at or near Keith or Grange crossroads. Their OB was near Newtack Farm at NGR NJ 461542. There was also a section at Huntly with an OB at NGR NJ 511338. Clearly there must have been many more sections in Morayshire however, for example at Forres, Lhanbryde, Spey Bay, Buckie, and so on the locations of which are now unknown. Care must be taken, when considering the matter, to differentiate between Regular, Home Guard and Auxiliary units as their locations were kept apart and in the case of the Auxiliary units they were a closely guarded secret. A rifle range used by Auxiliary units was pinpointed at St. John's Mead NGR NJ 012550, which was used by both Darnaway and Spynie sections. Both Home Guard and Auxiliary units used another range east of Pluscarden Abbey NGR NJ 145577 and at Blairmore Home Farm NGR NJ 4339 used by sections in training.

It is reported that the Darnaway section was involved in an episode when two German agents were captured near Mundole. They appear to have been spotted making their way down the River Findhorn and when they reached a quarry they lit a fire and the smoke gave away their location enabling the section to surround and capture them then handing them over to the Police at Forres Town Hall. All sections 'stood-to' on the 7th September 1940 when 'Cromwell,' the codeword signifiying 'Invasion Imminent,' was issued, but no other local alerts are recorded and unlike other areas such as the south of

England evidence of enemy activity was almost non existent although Home Forces were everywhere seen to be active. (Wilmot.1952:52)

Encouraged to live off the land where possible some members of the Spynie section, on one occasion, used some of their explosives on a fishing expedition on a local river, an episode that resulted in a confrontation with a senior officer at Home Guard HQ at 'Rotha' in Elgin. The incident was not repeated, at least by the Spynie section. One exercise they carried out consisted of the men being taken to the Tap O'Noth and being left there to find their own way home across country. On another occasion they started from Palmer's Cross, by Elgin, for a dummy attack on Bogs of Mayne airfield. By these and similar methods the training continued to engage the interest of the men and bring their skills to a peak of efficiency.

Finally

The Auxiliary units were 'stood down' and disbanded along with the Home Guard in November 1944. Why was this disbandment so long delayed when it was clear that Hitler had abandoned operation SEALION on 15 September 1940? There are several possible reasons, for example, it was known that the Germans continued to study and plan for SEALION, even carrying out invasion exercises, indicating that perhaps invasion was only postponed and not irrevocably abandoned pending the result of operation BARBAROSSA.

Again, the Auxiliary Units were employed increasingly to mount testing exercises against the defences manned by Home Forces to test their alertness. As 'D' day of operation OVERLORD approached the signals section communication net was particularly active taking part in the radio deception plan of operation FORTITUDE. Churchill needed to ensure the firm establishment of American 'lend lease' and the continued existence of the Home Guard and the Auxiliary units gave weight to the impression that the invasion continued to be a threat. There was a possibility that the deployment of Hitler's terror weapons the V1 and the V2 might have led to the supposition that the invasion could be mounted when these weapons came into action in June 1944.

As the forces for OVERLORD began to be designated and began their specialised training for the invasion of France, Home Forces were relieved of various duties by Home Guard units, such as guarding vital installations and so on. Many anti-aircraft and coastal defence batteries were also manned by the Home Guard. The maintenance of these forces was good for morale and until OVERLORD was launched and seen to be a success it was still felt that the possibility, however remote, of invasion by the enemy could not be ignored.

It should not be forgotten that the members of the Auxiliary Units were volunteers or were 'volunteered' for a job that was perceived as particularly hazardous and could so easily have been so. Their life expectancy was reckoned at 10-14 days. They endured long years of, what must have seemed at the time, boring and repetitive duties, attaining and maintaining a standard of discipline and efficiency which, had it been put to the test, would undoubtedly have proved a very nasty surprise for the enemy.

With the passage of time, and it is now more than half a century ago, the history of the Home Guard and the Auxiliary Units may seem somewhat unreal. Our memories may be influenced by the antics of 'Captain Mainwaring' and his men of the TV version of 'Dad's Army' and no doubt among the serious business there were light hearted incidents. Nevertheless, at their 'stand-down' in November 1944 nearly two million Home Guards demonstrated by their numbers alone that Home Guarding had been a serious business. Churchill recognised this in his minute of 7 January 1944 to the Secretary of State for War in which he said, 'we should make every effort to ease the lot of the Home Guard whose duties are more exhausting than any form of civil defence...many of these men have had little free time for more than three years'. (Churchill. 1944:599). Two million men equates roughly to 130 Infantry Divisions, a serious business indeed and one which might so easily have become deadly serious.

Although spread thinly over the country there is no doubt that the Home Guard could have made a real contribution to the defence of their homes and loved ones in the event of invasion. Compared with the regular Home Guard the Auxiliary Units estimated at 3,500 men were a small force but their estimated potential against the enemy could probably have been proportionately much greater. Their rewards were meagre with little no acknowledgement or thanks. It was and remained top secret and it is only now with the lapse of time that their story can be told with due appreciation of the part played by these men and women.

Home Guard Sub-Artillery

The generally acute shortage of weapons in Britain after Dunkirk in 1940 was particularly noticeable among the ranks of the Home Guard. In a speech on Home Guard affairs in December 1941 Winston Churchill reported that, where rifles were not available, efforts were being made to provide simpler hand-held weapons such as 'pike or a mace'. Orders were issued for the production of 25,000 pikes made of long metal tubes with bayonets welded on one end. Received with incredulous scorn by Home Guard units, they only served to raise questions like *"what about bows and arrows?"*

Inventive minds were, however, at work on developing more useful weapons such as the Northover Projector which fired grenades. Despite Churchill's personal endorsement of the weapon, which began mass production in October, (with over 8,000 issued by August 1941) the Home Guard did not take kindly to it, described by one of them as 'a piece of drain pipe on three legs'.On the general principle that 'beggars can't be choosers' the Home Guard was the repository of weapons rejected by the army. A weapon invented by W.H. Smith, a retired major, and called the 'Smith Gun; was ordered in 1941 and 4,000 were issued to the Home Guard by the summer of 1942. With a low muzzle velocity and a limited range of only 100 - 300 yards, it was reported as heavy and awkward to handle and quickly acquired a reputation for lack of safety. As one of the Home Guard commanders put it, "it has a terrifying reputation of killing its crew". With the passage of time it seems to have been well enough received by some units whilst others considered it a "junk weapon".

It was a bizarre device, which could be towed on its integral steel wheels behind a car. On arrival at its destination the gun was turned on its side, with one wheel forming the base and the other wheel as a shield against shrapnel or, at least, the rain. The gun was smooth bore, 75mm, and fired a finned projectile some few hundred metres. It was prominent and clumsy and seemed to have no virtues over a mortar of the same calibre.

Lieutenant Colonel L.V.S.Blacker, a T.A. Gunner Officer, invented a spigot mortar, but it was rejected by the War Office in 1939. Blacker modified his mortar design which was demonstrated to Churchill in August 1940 as a combined anti-tank and bombardment weapon. This was enthusiastically received by Churchill, who ordered its production on a scale of one Blacker Bombardment per Home Guard company.(See Appendix 4) Its obvious drawbacks were its weight of 360 lbs , an agonisingly slow rate of fire, a fierce recoil of 20 tons per square inch and the fact that it had to be dismantled to be moved. It was difficult to resight after the first bombs had been fired. Nevertheless, it seems to have had a brief positive effect on the morale of troops still chronically short of personal small arms. The Spigot Mortar, as it came to be called, had an anti-tank and an anti-personnel capability and it was accepted that its primary role would be as an ambush weapon. Tactically pre-sited in a well concealed position, the objective was to score a direct hit with the first shot - as the gun crew were unlikely to get a second chance. This was despite the fact that the instruction manual states that "single rounds do not give a true range result for which a group of five rounds is required".

This piece of sub-artillery comprised a short barrel of 29mm tube with, inside it, a heavily loaded spring steel rod - the spigot, which could be triggered to strike a charge on the end of the missile which was then projected towards the target. Each mortar had a crew of five. Designed to be mounted on four legs which fitted into sockets, the mounting could not adapt to the slope of the ground. A permanent mounting on a concrete pedestal, suitably reinforced, was therefore preferred.

The 20 lb anti-tank bomb was 26 inches long by 6 inches diameter, and had a range of 75 - 200 yards, or a theoretical maximum of 450 yards. The rate of fire was normally 6 rounds per minute. The 14 lb anti-personnel bomb measured 24 inches long by 4 inches diameter. The maximum range was 950 yards and the rate of fire was normally 8 rounds per minute. Both bombs had finned tails on which the true flight of the bomb depended, and which had a nasty habit of being flung back towards the gun crew when the bombs exploded. By the start of 1942 the Home Guard had been issued with 18,919 Northover Projectors, 3,049 Smith guns and 18,691 Spigot mortars.

A base plate for the Spigot mortar can be seen inthe South East corner of the Knockmasting Wood beside the road between Bilbohall and Mayne Farm, Elgin at map reference NJ 205617. This appears to have been designed for surrounding with concrete, but this has not been completed in this case. No trace remains of the trenches which were recommended for the gun crew.

Fig 15. Spigot mortar baseplate
(See also Appendix 5)
Photo: W A B

WORLD WAR II
IN MORAY

PART THREE

AIR

Part Three

Air

The Royal Air Force

The years following the First World War were lean times for the RAF when Britain relied almost exclusively for her defence on the Navy and left the Army and the Royal Air Force to deal with minor revolts in the colonies. It was in Iraq that the then Squadron Leader Arthur Travers Harris realised the possibilities of exerting punishing power from the air. He was an exception; not in his outlook but in his numbers. Pilots were few and far between and one year only three hopefuls were accepted for pilot training. One, who was successful, told how he counted the steps up to the interview room and was able to give the correct answer when asked how many there were. However, despite the low numbers enlisted as pilots, when called upon to expand, the RAF rose smoothly to the occasion. This was due to Lord Trenchard, who, in collaboration with Winston Churchill had prepared a far sighted plan in 1919 to have a small, highly skilled force, which could be quickly expanded if so required. By March 1932 the percentage of the gross national product spent on defence fell to 2.5%.. and the Air Force was at its lowest ebb. Next year, Adolf Hitler came to power in Germany and the drums of war started to beat, but so softly that, to start with, few heard them. Churchill was a notable exception, even though his figures for German rearmament were much exaggerated.

Even during the lean years the RAF showed the flag round the world. In 1928-1929 it evacuated 590 people of various nationalities from the British Legation at Kabul which was surrounded by hostile tribesmen. The Air Force won the Schneider Trophy for high speed flying in 1927, 1929 and 1931, thus gaining the trophy outright for Great Britain, but, more importantly, ensuring that the development work on the Rolls Royce engine would ensure that the Spitfire would be powered by the famous Merlin engine.

Fig 16. A recruiting poster
HMSO

As the thirties progressed so did the threat of war and Britain reluctantly, but deliberately, prepared for it. The recent examples from Spain and the British colonial experience had shown the uses and abuses of air power so an expansion of the RAF, though still hindered by the demands from the Navy, was set in motion. The Midlands of England could make the aircraft but the training of the pilots required clear skies and open spaces and these were limited in the south. However, beyond the Grampian mountains lies the Moray Firth littoral and this is where the climate is most favourable. The average annual rainfall is 62cm and this compares with 74cm in London while the annual sunshine is comparable to places much further south, such as the Humber. Despite the incidence of sea haar in the spring the number of days with fog and snow, both interdictive of flying, are low. Add to these advantages the then remoteness of Moray from Germany and Moray, as well as the rest of the low lying area round the Firth, became a favoured location for airfields.

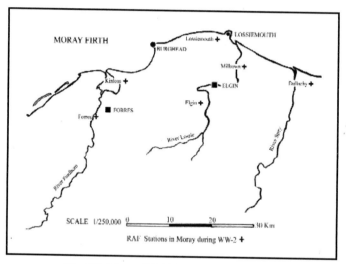

Fig 17. Map of RAF stations in Moray.
Map: I K

Kinloss and Lossiemouth became the first two of the eventual six airfields which were constructed on the flat lands of the Laich of Moray. Work started in 1937 and No. 14 Flying School at RAF Kinloss, which opened on 1st April 1939, exactly 21 years since the formation of the Royal Air Force. Lossiemouth, No.15 Flying School, opened a month later and both stations are still in active RAF service. Although Lossiemouth opened as a military airfield in 1939 the area had been accustomed to flying, as Ramsay Macdonald, even as early as his first premiership in 1924, used to fly from London to Lossiemouth and return in RAF aircraft.

The Royal Air Force had two respectable parents, the Army and the Navy, who, alas, did not love their offspring. For most of the war the Navy routinely fired at RAF aircraft which flew over their ships and eventually desisted from this unfriendly activity only when all the aircraft in the sky were either British or American. The Army, often delegated to guard RAF camps, resented the higher pay and better conditions enjoyed by the RAF personnel and reacted accordingly, i.e., badly. There were 2,600 operational aircraft and 174,000 men in the Air Force on 3rd September 1939 and 1,079,835 men, with an additional 182,000 WAAF (Womens' Auxiliary Air Force) in service in 1945. Contrary to popular thought, most flying crew were not officers but were non-commissioned, sergeants and flight sergeants, but whatever the rank, the pilot of the aircraft was the captain or skipper. However, once on the ground normal distinctions of rank were observed and there was seldom social interaction between commissioned and non-commissioned crew. Any which did occur took place on neutral territory, such as a local pub.

Bomber Command was subject to a rare disease, which only affected non-commissioned officers. It rarely attacked warrant officers and was never observed in commissioned crew. This was the dreaded Lack of Moral Fibre. There was only one symptom; a reluctance, developing into a refusal to take part in any further flying operations. It was believed to be contagious and there being no cure, the treatment was to remove the sufferer from the scene and post him to somewhere unpleasant, reduce him to the ranks, and set him to work cleaning out the latrines.

At the start of the war, Flying Schools were intermediate stations between the twenty Elementary Flying Training Schools and the Group Pools which provided advanced training to air crew prior to joining operational squadrons. By the spring of 1940 the Group Pool system was abandoned and Operational Training Units (OTU's) were introduced and these continued to function until the end of the war. At both Kinloss and Lossiemouth the initial principal training aircraft was the Oxford. The Airspeed Oxford was the RAF's standard multi-engined trainer. It was twin engined and, in its most popular mark, had 375hp Armstrong Siddeley Cheetah X engines. It was not an easy aircraft to fly but it was reckoned that this was a plus point as the pilot who could master the Oxford could go on confidently to fly any of the heavier bombers. Unfortunately, flying training results in accidents and despite the RAF's constant safety propaganda, including Bomber Command's excellent training magazine, 'Tee Emm', Pilot Officer Prune and his colleagues continued to prang valuable aircraft. As Prune, a cartoon character, who distinguished, or rather disgraced, himself on every issue of 'Tee Emm', commented "A good landing is one you can walk away from." It was not long before Nos. 14 and 15 Flying Schools reported their first accidents. In September 1939 two aircraft crashed at Kinloss, with a total of three dead, but as the war had started no mention of this appeared in the local papers. At Lossiemouth on 1st August, two Oxford aircraft collided near the Boar's Head rock and, this still being peactime, the local press was able to report the accident very fully.

In the spring of 1940, No.14 FTS left Kinloss and was replaced by No.19 Operational Training Unit which was equipped with Whitleys for heavy night bomber instruction. In addition to becoming a semi-operational station, Kinloss became home to No.45 Maintenance Unit which repaired a variety of aircraft. The Whitley, manufactured by Armstrong-Whitworth, first entered service with the RAF in March 1937. It was one of the first heavy night bombers and had the new stressed skin fuselage. It was powered by two Rolls-Royce Merlin engines and had nose and tail gun turrets and carried a crew of five. By 1940 it was becoming obsolescent as a front line bomber and by 1942 it was reduced to training and glider towing. It was not a particularly loved aircraft, unlike its contemporary, the Wellington, which affectionately known as the Wimpey, served as a front line aircraft for the whole of the war. Kinloss was an extremely busy airfield and early in May 1941 it hived off 'D' Flight of 19 OTU to a new satellite airfield at Balnageith on the outskirts of Forres and this was followed by 'C' Flight later the same year. The Whitleys were ancient and passing from one inexperienced pilot to another, accidents were tragically plentiful. According to 'The Whitley File' there were some 113 Whitley crashes associated with 19 OTU. Most crashes were "write-offs" and involved injury or death to the crews. The first was aircraft N1387 which was attached to 77 squadron and, having been on a sortie to Trondheim, ran out of fuel over Grantown and crashed there. An eyewitness describes how the aircraft clipped the top of some trees and crashed partially into the Spey before bursting into flames. The last was on 17th October 1944 when AD 685 lost control in cloud over East Marton in Yorkshire and subsequently crashed.

The most spectacular accident and one, alas, as tragic as any, occurred on 7th November 1940 when Whitley N1440 nose dived from 1,200ft into Forres. Miraculously no civilians were killed but the six crew were not so fortunate. The crash site is now a car park, but was once the garden of Fern Villa, just to the south of the High Street and adjacent to Tolbooth Street. A commemorative plaque was erected on the adjacent building in 1998. A random and equally tragic accident occured on 22nd February 1942 when LAC (Leading Aircraft Man) John Heywood Potts, who was billeted at Sanquhar, took a lift from an aircraft flying from Kinloss to Forres. The aircraft was making a turn when the inside engine failed and it crashed into the Findhorn. LAC Potts now lies in grave 27, row 'A' at Kinloss Abbey War Cemetery.

It is easy to think of these crashes as interesting statistics; but behind every one lies several human tragedies. Most of the crews were in their early twenties, several still in their teens and they had come, not only from all over the British Isles but also from Australia and Canada or even from Poland and Czechoslovakia. The following sad story is 'lifted' from Ted Hutchinson's 19 OTU, RAF Forres, memories. Ted arrived at Kinloss in March 1940 as a corporal and was demobbed in 1946 as a Flight Sergeant, having served practically all his war time service on the same station. Ted remembers one such occasion, 'a WAAF driver reported seeing a young woman crying on a banked roadside near the Forres camp. It turned out that she was the wife of a crew member killed in the previous night's crash: she had arrived in Forres to spend a few days with him. The WAAF returned to comfort her and to make sure that she safely returned to her hotel.'

A somewhat lighter incident occurred at RAF Forres when the local police inspector, John Ross, became concerned about the lax state of security. One night he clambered over the fence and went from parked aircraft to parked aircraft, writing on each with chalk 'Inspector John Ross Forres Police'. Next day his 'phone was ringing as he entered his office and he was able to explain to the agitated commanding officer that he had found no guards as he went round the aircraft. The luckless guards who had been idling away their time asleep or playing cards in their hut were all placed on charges.

Coincidentally not long after this incident the RAF Regiment was formed, initially to defend airfields with RAF personnel but eventually to become a crack fighting and ceremonial force. Diversions from OTU and maintenance routines were many and varied. As well as offering a temporary home to 77 Squadron it also provided space for other aircraft, for a time including Spitfires. In September 1941, Kinloss became the temporary base for 90 (Flying Fortress) Squadron, normally resident at Polebrook, Northampton. Their target was the battleship Admiral Von Scheer, then anchored in Oslo harbour. Two missions were attempted but both ended in failure and with them the RAF's faith in the Flying Fortress. Further attacks were made later in the war and these were eventually spectacularly successful.

Next year, in the spring of 1942, 35 Squadron, equipped with Handley Page Halifaxes, roosted at Kinloss, before taking off to bomb the Tirpitz, then anchored in a Norwegian fjord. The attacks were not successful. In the same year, OTUs throughout the country were combed to make up the magic number 1,000 for massive raids on Cologne and Bremen. 19 OTU sent twelve Whitleys, with their under training crews, to Abingdon en route for Germany. Only eleven returned, no doubt considerably more experienced than when they left Kinloss. However, despite occasional losses to the enemy, the major causes of aircraft accidents were domestic; pilot error, bad weather, unforgiving terrain and worn out aircraft all contributed. It is not known what category of accident was blamed for the distinctly odd happening on the evening of 19th October 1943 at Forres. A Whitley pilot was starting his run for take-off when he felt a heavy bump. Assuming a burst tyre he aborted and was then told by his wireless operator that he could see a wheel through his astro-dome. An incoming Anson had landed neatly and accurately on to the back of the Whitley, thus giving a whole new meaning to the expression 'piggy-back.'

Forres airfield was abandoned in October 1944 and the buildings were then used by Prisoners of War and were subsequently handed over to the Polish Army. Before leaving Forres, three 'D' Flight Whitleys, flown by experienced pilots, beat up the domestic site at less than 20 ft (6m). As they cleared the scene, other Whitleys followed them at not much greater height. Fortunately there were no casualties from this exhibition of skill and bravado.

A few miles along the coast to the east lies the airfield of Lossiemouth, which, like Kinloss is still operational. In the spring of 1940 the German invasion of Norway brought Lossiemouth into the war zone so 15 Flying School was despatched to Middle Wallop and was replaced by No.20 Operational Training Unit. As at Kinloss, a Maintenance Unit, No.46 MU, like a cuckoo in a nest, took up what the operational people considered to be valuable hangar space RAF Lossiemouth received early attention from the Luftwaffe and on 26 October 1940, doctor, then a student, John C.M.MacDonald was working in his garden in Elgin at dusk when he heard the distinctive note of a German aircraft. He looked up and saw the crosses on a low flying aircraft which was closely followed by two Spitfires. The intruder was shot down and the crew, who were buried with full military honours, lie in Lossiemouth cemetery. There were subsequent raids with civilian casualties but more deaths were caused by crashes of friendly aircraft. On 27th February 1945 a Wellington crashed at Seatown, Lossiemouth killing all of the crew except one and just after the war in Europe had ended, another Wellington crashed at Church Street, Lossiemouth, killing the three crew and eight civilians.

At the height of its use the airfield at Lossiemouth extended as far as Salterhill, some one mile (1.5km) south of the existing airfield where there are still some remains of the dispersal areas. There was also a 'pundit' stationed there. Pundits were high intensity flashing lights, which were used to give guidance to aircraft during conditions of poor visibility.

Fig 18. 20 OTU Crest at Bogs o' Mayne
Photo: A B Loveland

68

20 OTU was equipped with Wellingtons and Ansons. The Anson was similar to the Oxford but somewhat bigger and more powerful. But the Wellington was a darling, both to her crews and ground staff. Designed by Barnes Wallis of Vickers, Tallboy and bouncing bomb fame, it was built using a unique geodetic construction for the fuselage. This was covered in doped Irish linen and the whole made a cheap and easily repairable structure. The Wellington could absorb more flak than any comparable aircraft and its record of duty, having entered service in the RAF in 1938 until its final demob. in 1953 is only equalled by the length of service of the Shackleton. The Wellington went through many Marks. There was even one which had a metal water pipe welded along the length of the fuselage, the better to cope with heavy bomb loads. It carried a crew of five and ten times as many Wellingtons were built (11,461) as Whitleys.

Fig 19. Wellington X 1944-45
Photo: Alex Fraser

The high level of activity at Lossiemouth was such that by mid-summer 1940 a satellite airfield at Bogs o' Mayne or Manbeen, near Elgin, was opened. This was dangerously close to rising ground to the south and the plantation at Thomshill, two km. from the airfield was known to the pilots as Gremlins' Roost. Three years later an additional site at Milltown, to the east of Lossiemouth, was added and this became host to 'C' Flight. 20 OTU. Milltown, though a war-time airfield with no pedigree, took part in the eventual successful sinking of the great German warship, the *Tirpitz*.

An earlier unsuccessful attempt to sink the *Tirpitz* involved the Stirling bomber known as 'MacRobert's Reply'. Lady MacRobert was a wealthy widow who lost her eldest son in a flying accident in 1938 and who had the tragedy to lose her remaining two sons in the RAF in 1941. She then donated £25,000 to pay for a Stirling bomber which was ceremoniously named 'MacRobert's Reply'. Unfortunately the 'reply' ran off the runway at Lossiemouth and was so badly damaged that it had to be written off. Much longer lasting than the Reply is the charitable fund, bearing the MacRobert name, which is still in existence and still carrying out good work.

Having tried in 1943 with midget submarines and failing to sink the *Tirpitz*, in 1944 the Russians and Fleet Air Arm had a go at bombing and RAF planes took off for Russia, there to re-fuel and service their aircraft before heading for their target. The effect of this last attack was to cause the Germans to move the *Tirpitz* up to Tromsö Fjord. Tromsö was filled with refugees from the north of Norway who had been evacuated by the Germans as they retreated down Norway carrying out a scorched earth policy as they went. So it was important that any bombing be carried out in daylight and in good visibility. Not very common conditions, north of the Arctic Circle in early winter.

On the evening of the 28th of October 1944, three Moray airfields acted as overnight hosts for 36 Lancaster bombers. There were 14 of 9 Squadron dispersed to Kinloss, ten of 617 (Dambuster) Squadron found a home at Lossiemouth while another 16 of that famous Squadron had to put up with the more meagre comforts of Milltown. Low cloud and bad visibility hampered the operation but all the aircraft returned safely from Norway to Scotland except for one Lancaster, which landed in neutral Sweden. By November 11th the daylight window was fast closing and 32 modified Lancaster bombers rested and refuelled at Kinloss, Lossiemouth and Milltown and at 3a.m. on the 12th the Merlin engines roared at full revs as the heavily laden aircraft staggered off from the somewhat too short runways and turned north east to Arctic Norway. When they arrived over the target the weather was clear and fine and despite the danger from the high mountains flanking the *Tirpitz*, two tallboy bombs hit the target with several other near misses. The result was that the mighty *Tirpitz* rolled over with the consequent death of some 1,100 Kriegsmarine.

This was the apogee of the RAF presence in Moray. There was to be a fierce rearguard action by Germans in Norway against aircraft flying out from Dallachy, but the need for the bread and butter training of aircrew by 19 and 20 OTUs was no longer necessary. Dallachy, on the east bank of the Spey, was built during 1942/3 and one of its domestic sites was built on top of the alleged Roman Camp at Roman Camp Gate. Originally intended for Coastal Command, Dallachy was lent to Flying Training Command and from 25th June 1943 there was practically continuous flying by Oxfords. On 1st September 1944 Coastal Command took over and Beaufighters arrived in October to pursue the U-boats which had moved from their bases in France to Norway. Their first operation was on the 25th October, but due to bad weather this was cancelled. Many operations were to be aborted during the winter of 1944/45, which produced particularly heavy snowfalls and low temperatures in January. February brought some milder weather and on the 9th February, soon to be known as 'Black Friday',(see map at Appendix 2), 31 Beaufighters left Dallachy to harass enemy shipping along the Norwegian coast. Whether by intelligence or ill luck they met a squadron of Focke-Wulf 190's and nine

Beaufighters failed to return home. Several of those that did manage to stagger home were badly shot up and the wounded survivors were taken to Dr.Gray's hospital in Elgin where surgeon Gordon Scott operated while his wife, Dr. Mora Scott, was the anaesthetist.

The last official operation from Dallachy took place on 21st May 1945 when Beaufighters supervised the surrender of U-boats in the Norwegian fjords. Squadrons 144 and 455, which had been stationed at Dallachy, were disbanded and Squadrons 404 and 489 went to Banff. In November 1945 the station was put on a Care and Maintenance status and was eventually abandoned by the RAF. One of the domestic sites lay abandoned for years and trees were eventually planted over it and these, in turn, gave way to a minor housing development, thus effectively denying any possibility of establishing whether the Roman military had decided, two thousand years earlier than the RAF, that this was a good place to have a camp.

At its peak in early 1944 there were some 12,000 RAF personnel in Moray. Most of these were young men; aircrew exclusively so, whose life expectancy was not very high. This was something which had not seemed obvious in the earlier part of their training, because, being young, they still considered themselves immortal. By 1944, most initial flying training took place in Canada, where the good summer weather and the wide open spaces made for safe and ideal flying. Conditions were entirely different when they returned to the UK for further training at an OTU. Congested skies and bad weather, in unholy alliance with overworked aircraft, led to a high attrition rate and that was before the significance of Bomber Command's nominal casualty rate of 5 % sank in. Five per cent casualty rate means a 95% survival rate, reasonable odds under any circumstances. The devil was in the detail, and the little detail was that a crew must complete 30 operations before it was taken off duty. And, an operation had to be complete. It was no use dropping bombs somewhere over Germany and claiming a successful mission. Automatic cameras and synchronised flares meant that if the aircraft did not reach the target area then the flight was not counted towards the magic thirty.

One result of so many young men facing death was an instinctive desire to procreate. Weddings became popular and ex-officio couplings even more so. Frightening films on the more spectacular results of venereal disease were shown and dubious establishments were discreetly closed down. Entertainments were put on to distract the troops and establishments such as the Elgin Museum flourished. Attendance during the war years reached record heights, which have never been duplicated since.

The RAF and the WAAF (Women's Auxiliary Air Force) selected mainly personnel who had secondary education. Except for Air Gunners, this was exclusively so for aircrew. But ground crew too had to have high educational standards. The average time to train a wireless mechanic was twelve months and it was no use trying to instruct somebody in the complexities of wireless who did not already have a sound knowledge of mathematics. This concentration of talent meant that the authorities could not treat the airmen and airwomen as they might treat privates in the army. So, it was no coincidence that the RAF had smart uniforms with collar and tie while the army had shapeless battledress. Such small differences, amongst others, led to friction and this occasionally boiled over into fighting. During the early stages of the war the army defended the airfields in Moray and by 1942 there was almost a state of continual war between the services at Lossiemouth. These, and other incidents elsewhere, caused the Air Ministry to establish the RAF Regiment. Founded in the autumn of 1942, this was essentially a ground force fighting unit, integral with the RAF, which took over from the army the onerous duties of airfield defence.

But there was more to running an Air Force than just keeping the aircraft in the air. Crash sites, of which there were plenty, had to be visited and the dead and wounded removed, as well as the guns and ammunition. At first this was carried out by ad hoc groups of airmen and, subsequently by the RAF Regiment in the early autumn of 1942. However, with more crashes occurring on high ground in Scotland and Wales specialised Mountain Rescue Teams were set up at Kinloss and South Wales later in 1942. Today there are now two teams in Scotland and four elsewhere in the U.K. Each team consisted of six men, with others on stand-by, who continued with their ordinary duties until required to attend at a crash.

In December 1944 a particularly gruesome accident occurred in South Wales. An LAC was checking the Mountain Rescue packs. He had examined five and in each case the Verey pistol was, quite properly, found to be unloaded. As he pulled out the 6th pistol a WAAF entered the room and he playfully pointed the pistol at her and squeezed the trigger. The gun was loaded and the WAAF opened her lips to scream. The incandescent flare entered her open mouth and she died in agony a few days later. In this age, as sixty years ago, the basic rules still apply. Never handle a weapon without previously checking to see if it is loaded and never ever point a gun at anybody, unless you intend to use it.

But crashes were not limited to the land. Training aircraft also had a deplorable tendency to fall into the Moray Firth. There was no dedicated Air Sea Rescue Flight stationed along the Moray Coast but there were a couple of rescue launches stationed at Lossiemouth. These were 63ft (19m) long with a cruising speed of 32mph and a top speed of 40mph and were directed to the scene of the accident by the Royal Observer Corps who had continuously manned posts along the coastline.

Following the cessation of hostilities in Europe the RAF started to melt away and this continued even faster after Japan surrendered. The first field to be abandoned was Forres, which was placed on a care basis on 22nd October 1944 and now little remains except a few very dilapidated buildings. Bogs o' Mayne, aka Elgin, was taken over on 28th July 1945 as a storage site for unwanted Lancasters and Harvards and was completely closed in 1947. Milltown limped along doing odd jobs such as transporting Czech forces back to their homeland and the RAF gave up control when Lossiemouth was handed over to the Navy in 1946. The return of the RAF in September 1972 was soon followed by the closure of the flying field and the erection of the aerials of 81 Signals Unit. Dallachy was put on to care and maintenance on 24th November. It's role as Strike Wing station is well reported. What was very little known then and is even less known now was its role as a training camp for spies where only German was spoken and German rations were eaten.

This chapter cannot do justice to the thousands who came to Moray to do their bit, whether in the cookhouse or the cockpit. For the WAAF it was particularly traumatic. Many were well educated ladies who volunteered or were conscripted and its spartan barrack conditions. There was just enough space between the beds for a small locker, but that refinement was not often available. There were approximately 2,000 members of the WAAF stationed in Moray. Early on in the war, WAAFs had carried out office or domestic duties and, initially, had managed the anti-aircraft balloons.

However it was quickly found that the girls did not have the physical strength to manage the balloons and they were soon taken off that duty. Later women were invited to take up technical work and though many were called, few were chosen. Here again the lack of strength became apparent and the author is aware of one case where a WAAF tightened up the spark plugs on an engine and, when the aircraft was on a test flight, the spark plugs started to shoot out of the engine like sparrows flying home to roost.

At that time, becoming pregnant, unless in possession of a wedding ring, was not a cause for celebration nor did it usher in a potential life of state handouts, but, out of wedlock, it was a most shameful occurrence and the authorities did their best to keep the WAAF compound separate from the RAF, using either physical separation or barbed wire, and sometimes both. Friday night was domestic night when WAAFs were confined to barracks and washed their hair and repaired their clothes. WAAFs who married would try and obtain some parachute silk to make their trousseau, but this desirable, or rather coveted, material was closely controlled. More freely available, particularly at Lossiemouth, was the unbleached Irish linen used to cover the frames of the Wellington. This, when bleached by exposure to sunshine made excellent table cloths and pillow cases.

For the ground staff theirs was a life of hard work and monotony and, for the aircrew it was a life too often short and unpleasantly terminated. Then there were the hundreds who left Moray, sometimes for the first time, to endure the delights of square bashing, followed by concentrated training and subsequent posting to the flat land of Lincoln or the not so exotic delights of the Western Desert or the jungles of Burma. For all who served it was indeed 'Per Ardua ad Astra'.

The Observer Corps

The origins of the Observer Corps may be found in late 1914 when the first organised system was devised for identifying and reporting enemy aircraft over the British Isles. Originally in the close vicinity of London but in an extended area in 1915 the police were instructed to report by telephone to the Admiralty any sightings of zeppelins or aircraft. Considered ineffectual the operation was taken over by the War Office in 1917 and new measures were implemented under the command of Maj.Gen. E B Ashmore. CB, CMG, MVO. The main problem seems to have been the difficulty of reliably passing reports due to the inadequacy of the telephone network. This was finally improved by 1918 as the war came to an end.

The outbreak of the Second World War found General Ashmore, now generally considered to be the founder of the Observer Corps, still in post and he set about rebuilding an observation network incorporating ideas that had been worked out and approved in 1925. The Observer Corps was formed initially with two groups. These new ideas included the formation of observation areas within which observation posts were set up. Posts were deployed as static units, normally between six to ten miles apart. They were connected by direct landline telephone, in clusters of three or four to one plotter at the operations room main plotting table in plotting centres established to collate and process the information gathered by the observers. As the Observer Corps expanded it was taken over by the Air Ministry from 1 January 1929. and Air Commodore E A D Masterman, CB, CMG, CBE, AFC, was appointed its first Commandant.To begin with the Corps' attention was centered in the areas around London, considered the probable focus of future enemy attention. But as Germany's intentions became clearer by the time of the Munich crisis in 1938 most of Britain was covered with a network of Observer Corps posts. Called out on 24 August 1939 the Corps had 40,000 observers already trained to provide a reliable early warning system. The HQ of the Corps was established at Bentley Priory at Stanmore in Middlesex in 1938. Air Chief Marshal Sir Hugh Dowding C-in-C Fighter Command took up residence there in July 1936 and began to organise the air defence of Britain with Fighter Squadrons, Anti-Aircraft Command, Balloon Command, RDF (later RADAR) Stations and the Observer Corps. An underground command bunker was built and manned from March 1940.

Observation posts were located in places where an uninterrupted view of the sky was possible. Usually high ground was preferred but if this was not possible then the tops of high buildings were used. The observers on duty had to remain in the open despite adverse weather and even sometimes despite enemy action. Each post maintained a Log of events. As the organisation grew the trained observers were given the responsibility of training new and less experienced members, so a post was often occupied by more than two observers.

The plotting table on a stand showed the map of the area. The instrument enabled the observer to estimate the height, track and position of the object sighted.

Fig 20. A Micklethwaite Height Corrector
Courtesy R Milne

The Micklethwaite Height Corrector is based on a mathematical formula, whereby the action of setting a height on the height scaled bar, together with the action of aligning an aircraft (or other overhead object) in the sights of the sighting arm, will move the pointer, which is part of the sliding carriage on the base line, so that the position of the aircraft is found in relation to the ground.

The Observer post was always manned by not less than two observers one of whom was equipped with a telephone headset and microphone and was in communication with the report centre whilst the other was equipped with a pair of powerful binoculars and gathered the intelligence about the aircraft, type, numbers of aircraft. nationality, height, course and present position which was passed to the first man to send on to the area report centre.

In order to minimise the disturbance created by air-raid alerts some posts adjacent to factories engaged on war work, often even on the roof of the building, had an alarm that they could sound if the raid came close enough to warrant the workers seeking shelter. If there was no local alarm the alert was ignored and work continued uninterrupted

The cinema and television has made most people aware of what the inside of a report centre looked like. There was a large centre table, marked off in squares, representing the centre's area around which there was a team of plotters with coloured markers they moved around in accordance with the information coming to them from the observer posts. On a raised area overlooking the table the tellers assessed the developing situation and issued orders to fighter squadrons under their command.

By 1943 as radio direction finding (RDF), or RADAR as it was later called, developed, the incoming aircraft were detected earlier, up to 100 miles away, and this information was also fed to the plotting table to supplement the observers' reports. The country was divided into groups, each with its own HQ and with main HQ at Bentley Priory. Group 13 covered the area north of a line through Church Fenton, NGR SE 5236 just east of Leeds including northern England and the whole of Scotland with its HQ at Newcastle, under the command of Air Vice Marshal Richard Saul.

13 Group Sector Stations were located at Turnhouse, Ackrington, Unsworth and Church Fentom. Each Sector Station Operations was under the command of a Controller. Within the Group there were designated areas. Morayshire was covered by Area 38, Banff, Aberdeen and Elgin with the Centre town at Keith. (PRO. AIR 2/1992)

> *In Morayshire observation posts were established as follows: (Wood.1976:331)*
>
> *Carron. At NGR NJ 228438.Opened Aug 1940; Resited at NGR NJ 235441 Sept. 1941; Undergrounded Jan 1962.*
>
> *Dallas, At NGR NJ 133525 Opened July 1940;*
> *Resited at NGR NJ 124530 Nov. 1953; Undergrounded Apr.1962.*
>
> *Elgin, At NGR NJ 213641 Opened July 1940; Resited at NGR NJ 184636 Jan 1953; Resited at NGR NJ 195608Nov 1959; Undergrounded Jan 1962.*
>
> *Findhorn, At NGR NJ 038649 Opened July 1940; Resited at 03556488 and Undergrounded Feb.1959.*
>
> *Grantown-on-Spey, At NGR NJ 022261; Opened July 1940; Resited at NGR NJ 031282; Undergrounded Nov.1962.*

In the late 50s and early 60s with the worsening relations with Russia and the advent of the Cold War most observer posts were put underground in secure bunkers with facilities which it was hoped would permit personnel to survive a nuclear attack and maintain surveillance and communications.

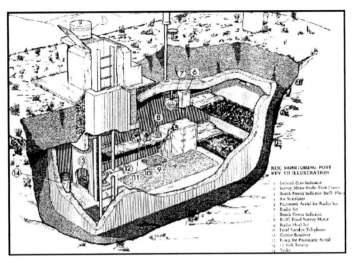

Fig 21. A RORC underground bunker c1960
Courtesy R. Milne.

In the early years of the Corps formation there was some uncertainty and debate about the status of Observers as well as the name of the unit, a debate that started in October 1935. Originally the men had joined as unpaid volunteers from patriotic reasons and for its close connection with the RAF. They had a status as special constables of which they were to be deprived (On the outbreak of war the connection between the Observer Corps and the Police with the observers being treated as special constables would be broken.) As late as August 1939 the question was still being debated as to whether the men should be treated as volunteer civilian personnel or as a service unit. So far as pay, discipline, uniform etc., was concerned it was thought they should be organised entirely on a civilian basis as it was at the start, or that it should become part of the RAFVR with commissioned officers and enlisted personnel. To have a mixture of the two would be fundamentally unsound. Eventually the decision was taken to treat the Corps as a service unit with conditions of employment, pay and discipline in line with the RAF. The hierarchy of the Corps being equivalent to RAF ranks. Starting with Observer equivalent to Aircraftman and rising by way of leading observer, chief observer, observer officer, observer lieutenant, observer lieutenant-commander and observer captain being equivalent to a Group Captain. Areas controlled by a commandant equated to an Air Commodore. These reforms were taking place under the command of Air Commodore Ambler who was returned to Fighter Command giving place to Air Commodore Finlay Crerar who remained in charge until November 1945. In order to ensure that every Observer Corps Centre and Post was continuously manned during war, by trained personnel physically capable of performing their duties the corps was instituted in two classes.

Class A was to comprise observers who were over 35 years of age, with good hearing and eyesight (with glasses if required) and who could give a guaranteed 56 hours a week for which they were paid an hourly rate, but no travelling or subsistence money

Class B was to be observers who could give a maximum of 24 hours weekly for three months. Payment to be similar to Class A.

Other appointments included Head Specials of Posts, Controllers and Assistant Controllers and a clerk for each centre and Officers. Those officers who had been retired from one of the services should be accorded their retired rank and be seconded to the Observer Corps. Other officers with no previous service were to be granted honorary commissions in the RAFVR in ranks ranging from Flight Lieutenant to Group Captain.

The role of the Observer Corps was simply defined. They were there to observe, identify and report enemy aircraft, acting as the nation's eyes and ears. On being observed and identified as enemy the aircraft was continuously monitored with its type, speed, course, height and nationality being reported by telephone to a report centre. From there the information went to Fighter Command Sector operations room which processed the information to alert relevant units of the air defence system, the RAF, Army and police and fire brigades. As the aircraft moved across country it was reported from post to post until it went out of sight.

The observation of the aircraft was not always visual. In conditions of cloud, fog, mist or other adverse weather conditions and at night the identity could only be made by sound. Observers were trained in a method of finding the height of an aircraft by sound alone. Fortunately most German aircraft had a very distinctive engine note. British aircraft had synchronised engines. On multi-engined machines all engines reached 'top dead centre' simultaneously. German aircraft were not synchronised, so in twin engined aircraft the engines operated at slightly different speeds giving rise to a distinctive beat note. Later in the war the invention and development of Radio Direction Finding (RDF) or RADAR together with electronic acoustic systems linked to AA gun batteries took most of the guesswork out of unsighted reporting.

With the defeat and occupation of Norway, Holland, Belgium and France the Nazis launched their operation 'Attack of the Eagles' which was their name for the attempt to obtain air supremacy over Britain prior to launching their invasion on operation 'Sea Lion'. By 31 July 1940 Britain had 39 fighter stations with 66 squadrons all with Spitfires, Hurricanes and Blenheims except for two squadrons which had Defiants. The Hurricane was the 'star', shooting down more than all the rest combined.

The Observer Corps had the problem of identifying various types of German aircraft. These were mainly, Me 109E (the 'Stuka'), and Me 110, JU 97B, He 111, JU 88A and Do 172. The Me's with their bright red and yellow paint and the 'gull wing' Stuka were easiest to identify as was the Dornier 172 nicknamed 'the flying pencil' due to its very slender fuselage. As well as tracking intruders the Corps also confirmed 'Kills' and losses and noted the position of downed British planes and crews. Later in the war this problem of correct identification of aircraft was made easier when friendly aircraft had broad white bands painted on the wings, the fuselage and the tail after 6th June 1944. '

Fig 22. An aircraft identification aid.
HMSO

On 9 April 1941 H M King George VI granted the title Royal Observer Corps. In September of that year women were enlisted in the Corps. Initially as clerks and for other sedentary work they soon began to serve, at their insistence, as observers. The RADAR operators were drawn from the Women's Auxiliary Air force (WAAF). Up to now the observers had worn mufti with an armband, but from June 1942 with A/C G. H. Ambler as commandant, the ROC adopted a uniform comprising an air-force blue overall with the observer corps badge, a dark blue mackintosh and a forage cap. Later the uniform was battledress similar to the standard RAF light blue but with a cloth ROC badge sewn onto the right breast, There was also a black beret with a ROC cap badge.

Life in the observer corps was very similar to life in any other of the military services. It consisted of long periods of boredom punctuated with brief periods of furious and often frightening activity. There was a boring period just after war was first declared when nothing much happened in place of the expected air raids. This was the period of the so-called 'phony war'. Next came the fury of the 'Battle of Britain' followed by the 'Baedecker Raids' on British cities. Most of this was confined to England, however, and so far as Morayshire was concerned there was only the occasional nuisance raid or reconnaissance incursion as the occupation of Norway brought Northern Scotland within range of enemy aircraft.

As the time for the invasion of Europe approached concern was being expressed about the increasing numbers of aircraft being shot down by 'friendly fire' in spite of the efforts of the Central School of Aircraft Recognition that had been set up to teach allied forces. Air Chief Marshal Leigh-Mallory discussed the problem with Air Commodore Crerar, Commandant of the ROC and identified a need for trained observers to advise gun crews on the defensively equipped merchant ships (DEMS) that would be used in large numbers during the invasion planned for June 1944. The call went out on 28 April 1944 to the trained observers of the ROC seeking volunteers to enter the Royal Navy for two months to serve on ships. The volunteers would continue to wear the ROC uniform with the addition of a SEABORNE shoulder flash and a Naval armband. Over 1300 volunteered and were formed into squadrons of two flights each of 15 men. After learning about Oerlikon guns and PAC Rockets with which the DEMS were equipped the observers were given a crash course in everyday naval matters ready for a life afloat.

In the event the enemy aircraft observed were few in numbers, as the Luftwaffe was kept in reserve, and the principal job of the seaborne observers was to restrain the trigger happy gun's crews from shooting down the Mustangs, Thunderbolts, Typhoons, Lightnings and Spitfires all of which carried the broad white identifying stripe on tail and fuselage. It was two and a half months before many of the seaborne observers returned to their land duties.(Buckton.1993:71)

Although it did not occur in Morayshire, an aircraft passing through the southern part of Group 31 was an example of the expertise acquired by the observers; this was the identifying and reporting of the flight of Hitler's Deputy, Rudolf Hess, to Scotland in 1941

On the night of 10-11 May there was a 500 bomber raid on London. Whilst this was going on a lone Messerschmitt was closing the coast off Holy Island, Northumberland, at 12,000 feet where it jettisoned its long-range fuel tanks. Radar began to track the incursion which was designated 'Raid 42' Within a quarter of an hour the aircraft was spotted by an Observer post of Group 30. At 22.35 the next post identified the aircraft, flying at an estimated 50ft, as a Me 110 and reported it to HQ Fighter Command of 13 Group located at Durham. Knowing that it was beyond its usual range and operating area the Controller discounted the report and considered it was probably a Dornier 17.

A misleading report from Radar reported the raid over the North Sea and it was assumed that Raid 42 had diverted. The track which continued westwards across Durham was redesignated 'Raid 42 J' As it continued on track the aircraft entered the airspace of Group 31 whose OPs continued to identify it as a Me 110 It was lost for a while in the Ettrick Forest vicinity until it was picked up again by 34 Group operating out of Glasgow. At 2245 the sound plot was confused by a Defiant scrambled from Prestwich to intercept the raider. Despite the RAF insistence on the Dornier 'ID', Glasgow designated it as unidentified or 'X Raid W,1'

The Glasgow plotters analysed the reports and calculated that the aircraft was travelling at over 300 m.p.h.., far too fast for a Dornier, moreover it was outpacing the Defiant. In spite of this the RAF ordered it to be redesignated as a Dornier 17. OPs were now instructed to try for a visual, the reverse of usual night procedure. Several posts confirmed the Me including West Kilbride where it was flying at only about 25 ft and the black cross markings were clearly visible. The RAF remained intransigent. Eventually, reaching the coast the aircraft went out to sea for the pilot to check his position and returning over the land at 13.09 the pilot was seen to eject and the aircraft crashed. The location was plotted by Post H.2.(Wood. 1975: 1-3 and PRO AIR 16 / L266). The Second World War finally ended with the surrender of Japan on 14 August 1945. The ROC took part in the London Victory Parade and with no longer the need to watch the skies over Britain the ROC was 'Stood Down'. As an integral part of the national defence system disbandment was not considered and with the 'Cold War' developing the Corps was rebuilt under the command of Air Commodore The Earl of Bandon vice A/C Crerar in November 1945.

Radar

RDF (Radio Direction Finding) or Radar, as it came to be called, was a war winning invention. Despite the fact that the Germans had invented the principle and demonstrated it as early as 1905 they failed to realise its potential as a weapon and did not develop it. It was left to Robert Watson Watt to develop it and by 1939 and the outbreak of World War Two RDF was already four years old and Britain's South and East coasts were covered with a series of installations called 'The Home Chain'. (HC stations).The stations were identified by a series if lattice steelwork transmitter masts each 350 feet high by means of which it was eventually possible working on 20-30 MHz frequency band to identify movement at long range up to 100 miles, although low flying aircraft could remain undetected.

The Germans sent a Zeppelin to fly along the South coast in 1939 in an attempt to establish the purpose of these masts but they were using the wrong frequency and gave up after the first attempt when their trial failed to provide any useful information. The early radar sets were too large to fit into aircraft and ships but by the end of 1941 a small magnetron-powered centimetric radar set was developed for the purpose. The development of these was the British contribution but with limited production capacity a deal was struck with the

Americans that in exchange for British know-how they would provide the productive capacity.

The Germans never made a determined effort to knock out the RDF stations, but there was one air raid that caused little damage and it was never repeated. The information gathered by these stations was passed to RAF Fighter Command that enabled selected squadrons to be airborne ready to meet the attack. It only took the enemy about five minutes to cross the English Channel whereas it took about thirteen minutes for a fighter plane to reach its operational height, so early warning of impending attack was of critical importance.

There was a RDF station set up on the hill south of Cummingston at NGR NJ 1468. It comprised seven masts and a collection of wooden huts. The site was surrounded by a security fence and guarded by the Home Guard. The radar sets were operated by WAAFs. The site has now been cleared and there are no remains of any significance.

Fig 23. A typical radar station
350' steel lattice mast
Photo: Dr M. Osborne

Burghead Radio Station

The radio station at Burghead was operational during the war. It was, and still is a relay station for the BBC. In those days the radio was always referred to as 'the wireless'. During the war the station began broadcasting programmes of the BBC Home Service on a 100 Kw transmitter. Later, in 1942, it had a second smaller transmitter of about 5 Kw capacity and began transmitting the Light Programme. To minimise the possibility of enemy stations pirating the British programmes in order possibly to broadcast their own form of subversive propaganda the British announcer always opened his programme by announcing his name. For example, 'This is the BBC Light Programme introduced by Alvar Liddell…' The voices and names of the announcers soon became familiar and easily recognisable to listeners. In fact the Germans never did try to use the British broadcasting system for their own ends although it was a form of psychological warfare practised extensively by the British. The Germans set up broadcasting stations purporting to be British, on the continent, for subversive propaganda prior to operation SEALION. These broadcasts were intended to cause panic and confusion on subjects such as spies, parachutists in disguise and the supposed existence of a fifth column.

To avoid radiation from the station assisting enemy aircraft in direction finding the broadcasting stations in Britain were shut down from time to time when enemy aircraft were in the vicinity. This was accomplished by a London Controller who sent out an 'Urgent Priority' signal to the stations affected. The shut down period usually lasted for about 15 minutes.

The Station had mains power but was equipped with stand by generators in case of supply failure. The station employed six engineers on each of three shifts over a 24 hour period. In addition there were others employed daily, an electrician, a rigger and three labourers together with a night watchman. The station was surrounded by a security fence and guarded by the Home Guard.

WORLD WAR II
IN MORAY

PART FOUR
DEFENSIVE
MEASURES

Part Four
Defensive Measures

On 10 May 1940, a Home Defence Executive was set up chaired by the C-in-C Home Forces, then from 27 May, by General (later Field Marshal Lord) Ironside. His resources for the defence of Britain's 400 miles (640 km) of threatened coastline were dangerously sparse. There was only one weak and incompletely equipped armoured division, together with 15 inexperienced infantry divisions averaging less than half their establishments, making a total fighting strength of 116,000 men. All divisions were desperately deficient of equipment, especially of artillery after so much material was abandoned by the BEF at Dunkirk. Of the total of only 963 tanks in the whole country many were awaiting repair or were obsolescent and 160 were armed only with machine guns. There was a general acute shortage of all other arms.

The defensive strategy adopted by Ironside was to hold the enemy on the beaches for as long as possible with defended obstacles while the best of the rest was mobilised for counter attacks. Inland, the country was divided into defensive zones by the construction of lines of obstacles. The most important was designed to protect London, the industrial heartland and the east coast as far north as Edinburgh and was designated the GHQ Line; other 'stop' lines subdivided this plan to protect key installations and to limit the extent to which the invader would be free to move about.

The GHQ Line used natural features wherever possible, such as rivers, railway cuttings and canals linked together with anti-tank ditches in the gaps between them. Where ditches could not be excavated other obstacles were contrived, mainly concrete blocks of various sizes supplemented where necessary by barriers of steel rails. Incorporated at intervals in the defensive lines were pillboxes positioned to give covering fire and to hold off infantry together with barbed wire and mines. Trees were felled in places where they could form a necessary obstacle. At the very beginning of the war barricades were made from whatever lay at hand or could be commandeered., but as time passed these flimsy makeshifts were replaced by more suitable and permanent obstacles. .

Pillboxes are still to be found at intervals along the defensive lines of concrete blocks lining the low lying sand and shingle beaches of Moray's coastline. Their purpose is clear, but there are other pillboxes in solitary positions, established to guard key points, surviving throughout the area. In some cases, however, due to topographical changes and changes in land use or development it is sometimes a puzzle to decide what the pillbox was originally designed to protect. As an important component of a static defensive strategy the pillbox was designed to accommodate a small number of men, 2 to 10, whose role was to give covering fire over an obstacle to prevent its easy removal. This was at best a delaying tactic whereby a series of defended obstacles would take the impetus out of an assault and reducing it with each encounter bringing it eventually to a halt where it could be finally overcome.

Pillboxes in that situation were vulnerable to attack. Each one had a blind side from which an assailant could approach unseen until near enough to lob a grenade through one of the weapon slits. Unless the pillbox was one of the larger ones with an internal blast wall this sort of attack was invariably successful. They were also vulnerable to attack from flame-throwers. The only way a pillbox might be expected to survive against a determined assault was if it was one of a complex of pillboxes all sited so that they could provide mutually supporting fire to each other.

Coastal Battery

After the German occupation of Norway in 1940 the emphasis on the danger of invasion of Britain shifted from the south coast of England to include the East Coast of Scotland. The long shallow sandy beaches facing the North Sea were obvious targets for invasion craft and measures were taken to put them into a state of defence. The beach between Lossiemouth and Spey Bay was regarded as particularly vulnerable and a coastal battery was constructed in the close vicinity of the 'Boar's Head' rock, north of Innes Links in the parish of Urquhart at NGR NJ 2558 6814 in 1941.

Fig 24. Gun emplacements and anti-tank blocks
Photo: W A B

The battery comprised two emplacements each armed with a 6" Mark XI gun on a Mark V mounting (J Dorman. *Pers Commn*), two searchlight emplacements, three engine houses and another emplacement, purpose unknown, but probably a control centre with rangefinder. There was a hutted camp for the troops of the 227 Coast Battery, 501 Coast Regiment Royal Artillery manning the battery. The battery guns had been scrapped by the Navy, after being removed from ships after the First World War, but happily kept for possible future use. The former fashion for open mountings with only a low parapet was found unsatisfactory with the advent of low-flying aircraft and a roof and front wall was now favoured.

As the war progressed and plans began to form for the eventual return to the continent of Europe it became clear that large numbers of troops would be required. Accordingly, since the danger of invasion had receded the War office in January 1942 gave authority for the Home Guard to take over duties at Anti-Aircraft and coastal Batteries. In June a unit to take over the battery at Innes Links was formed by the 1st Moray Battalion Home Guard. This new unit was designated 'E' Company and was mustered by late September / early October largely from men transferred from 'D' Company. The Officer Commanding was Capt. W A Mustard and his 2i/c was 2/Lt A K Mellenfield. Instructors from the Royal Artillery were attached for training the new unit.

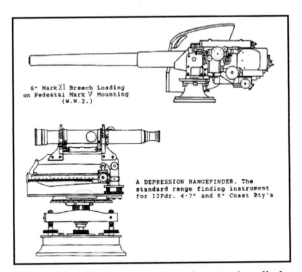

6" Mark XI Breech Loading on Pedestal Mark V Mounting (W.W.2.)

A DEPRESSION RANGEFINDER. The standard range finding instrument for 12Pdr. 4·7" and 6" Coast Bty's

Fig 25. The type of armament that was installed
Ref: J. Dorman (1996)

In February 1943 'E' Company took over the battery for a practice shoot and achieved a report as 'the best Home Guard Unit in the North of Scotland'. The battery was entirely manned by 'E' Company from the end of March 1943. In July 1943 it successfully passed an inspection by the RA and went on to win in a competition with an Inverness battery in 1944. In April 1945 the Unit was stood-down and the battery was put on a care and maintenance basis. It was removed later that year.

Other Defences

Wherever the many sand and shingle beaches of North East Scotland were deemed to offer a potential for a landing they were heavily defended with a varying assortment of devices intended to hinder the enemy from carrying the impetus of his initial assault to the hinterland. These devices included anti-tank and anti-personnel mines laid in the sand and attached as boobytraps or anti-handling devices on other obstacles. As a rule beach mines (code name 'toadstool') sat on a 15" square base and were about 6" high and contained about nine pounds of 'Amatol', or sometimes TNT. The mines were laid eight yards apart in eight rows giving a density of about one mine per yard of frontage. The mines were so sensitive that a rabbit could detonate them and many stray dogs suffered as a result. The beaches from the mouth of the River Deveron in the east to Nairn in the west were strewn with these deadly weapons.

Concealed flame-throwers that could incinerate an intruding craft in a wall of fire protected the entrances to the harbours. In Morayshire the main surviving beach obstacles appear to be lines of anti-tank concrete blocks with pillboxes interspersed at intervals to give protection for troops providing covering fire. It is difficult now to be sure where the barbed wire defences were placed but it is reasonable to assume that they would have been erected either before or in conjunction with the concrete blocks to deny ready access to infantry and soft skinned vehicles, neither is there any longer any evidence of the anti-air-landing poles that were set up in the open areas although there are still some witnesses who remember them.

Fig 26. Anti-tank blocks on Lossiemouth east beach
Photo: W A B

Elsewhere the beach defences included barriers of scaffolding poles boobytrapped with mines, but these do not appear to have figured largely, if at all, in Morayshire. Anti-tank ditches were hastily dug in many places, usually backfilled after the war. They leave little trace and none have been located locally.

Roads likely to be selected as approach routes for invading troops were provided with a variety of fixed and mobile obstacles guarded by pillboxes to give covering fire. These obstacles were frequently supplemented by concealed flame throwing (Flame fougasse) charges buried in the roadside verges.

Fig 27. Pillbox at East Road Elgin
Photo: W A B

The 'Flame fougasse' comprised 40 gallon (182-litre) drums containing a mixture of tar, lime and petrol, usually mounted in a battery of four. These were set up in the banks at bottlenecks, defiles or narrow points beside roads and lanes and could be detonated by steel filings propelled into the drum by a small explosive charge. They would project a fierce jet of flaming liquid designed to stick to anything it encountered. A simpler version was a Static Flame Trap comprising a tank of petrol installed above a dip in the road, which could be flooded with it whenever an enemy tank or vehicle appeared and it could be ignited by a Home Guard with a Molotov Cocktail or Very pistol.

It is interesting to note that similar fougasse devices were incorporated by the Germans into the fortifications of their West Wall. Another fire and flame experiment, by the Petroleum Warfare Department, called the Flame Barrage carried out on the shore of the Solent and at Studland Bay in 1941 to defend the beaches by literally setting the sea on fire and creating a marine inferno, was successful in the main but was too expensive in the use of the necessary materials. It is believed, however, that these spectacular experiments duly reported by agents to the Germans gave rise to a popular belief that Britain's coasts could be ringed with fire.

With the German occupation of Norway, the Scottish airfields suddenly became vulnerable. With its proliferation of airfields Moray was particularly vulnerable and extensive use was made of camouflage techniques. There was also an effort made to mislead the enemy by the establishment of a dummy airfield, or 'Q' field as it was designated. The ground defence of the airfields was still an army responsibility until the RAF Regiment was formed for the purpose. Churchill stressed the importance of RAF personnel being prepared to take part in airfield defence scheme by arming themselves with whatever weapons they could acquire or improvise. He said 'it should be clearly understood by all ranks that they are expected to fight and die in defence of their airfields'. Although the invasion never came the airfields were ringed with concrete defence posts, and barbed wire and dummy defence posts were mixed in with the real ones. Within the airfield rifle pits were dug round hangars and station buildings.

One innovative idea that was tried in 1940 was the 'Pickett Hamilton' retractable fort. This was a defence post designed to be sited on runways and dispersal areas flush with the ground and able to bear the weight of 6-7 tons if an aircraft passed over them. They were designed to be manned by two airmen with automatic weapons who would maintain a watch through a manhole and would raise the fort when an attack was deemed to be imminent. The fort could be raised about 3 feet above ground level by compressed air, hydraulically or by counterbalance in about 15 seconds.

These forts were installed by June 1941 in the North of Scotland at airfields in Wick, Castletown, Evanton, Lossiemouth, Kinloss, Dalcross and Skeabrae. Altogether a total of 170 had been installed at 59 airfields. But, there were several problems associated with them such as a tendency, in many places, to flood, necessitating constant pumping out. The crews would have to remain in place until flying operations had ceased and the forts would have to have ammunition replenished across open ground devoid of cover. Bomber Command considered the forts to be useless and by 1942 ordered building to cease.

Passive defence of all installations was supplemented by strict attention to camouflage especially from the air. Concrete runways were rendered less conspicuous by the addition of painted hedges and other features. Dummy or 'Q' airfields were set up in places. There was one at Roseisle in Morayshire. Some airfields, though only one in Scotland, were prepared for demolition in case of invasion.

With the reduction in the threat of invasion by April 1944 Churchill was saying that the maintenance of so many men in the RAF Regiment to guard airfields was no longer justified. He suggested that they should be reduced by the transfer of 25,000 to the Army, two thousand had already been transferred to the brigade of Guards in 1944.

WORLD WAR II
IN MORAY

PART FIVE

ALLIES

WORLD WAR II
IN MORAY

PART FIVE

ALLIES

Part Five

Allies

It was not just those born in these islands who served this country and the whole of humanity in these dark and troubled days. People, far from home and with little to encourage them, helped to defend this land. Poles, Czechs, Norwegians and Indians as well as the occasional German did their bit; now, alas mostly forgotten. But go to any War Graves Commission Cemetery in Moray and there you will see the graves of the men from Canada, Australia, Africa and New Zealand who volunteered to fly, to fight and eventually to die, for Britain. They died as men but so many were only boys in years, some only 18 or 19 years old. In October 1940 the approximate number of Allied military contingents in Britain were Polish 18,000; French 850; Norwegian 15,000; Dutch 1,500; Belgian 800; Czechoslovakian 3,000. In addition to the foregoing numbers there were Allied sailors and airmen and a few Danes, one of whom was awarded the Victoria Cross. (Fleming. 1957:65fn.). A Victoria Cross was also awarded posthumously to a second generation Italian whose father was released from internment camp to receive the medal at Buckingham Palace on behalf of his son.

The Poles

The Poles were the first to arrive when the remnants of their army escaped from the jaws of the Nazi and Soviet attacks. These early survivors were considerably augmented in the summer of 1940 with the arrival of more Polish troops who had escaped to France. These latter, after minimal training, were attached to Scottish Command and formed part of the defence of Scotland. Major parts of the Polish Air Force were reformed at Kinloss and several pilots distinguished themselves in the Battle of Britain later that year. By late 1942 there were further recruits, when prisoners, taken by the Soviets and sent to Siberia, were released into the Middle East and transported back to Britain. After training many of these soldiers were sent to Italy where several died in the infamous bloodbath at Monte Cassino.

There was a final influx of Poles and Ukrainians in mid summer 1944 when reluctant soldiers and forced labour recruits were taken prisoner at Normandy and shipped up to Scotland. No rations had been provided and the starving prisoners were decanted at Forres and promptly raided the adjoining field, eating raw the carrots and unripe potatoes. The Red Cross then intervened and provided money for the purchase of such unrationed food as was available. The prisoners were then separated and the Poles and some Ukranians, who could pass as Poles, were equipped in British battle-dress, given rudimentary military training and sent off to the front line.

The Norwegians

The Norwegians, who arrived in the summer of 1940, were in two groups, not mutually exclusive. There was the regular army and the shadowy home army who messed about in boats, mainly with a single cylinder diesel engine which had a very distinctive 'tonk, tonk, tonk', though it is whispered that several were also fitted with more powerful engines for emergency use. Boats from the Norwegian fishing fleet, which had managed to escape from Norway, were based at Buckie for the duration of the war and provided an excellent cover for the clandestine activities of their service compatriots. Buckie and the small ports of that corner of the Moray Firth became known locally as 'Little Norway'

By 20th June the majority of the Norwegian army was stationed at Dumfries, and so desperate was the shortage of weapons that a detachment of Norwegians paraded before Crown Prince Olaf, presenting arms with pikes. A few months later there was a detachment of Norwegian artillery at Rafford. The winter of 1940/41 was exceptionally cold and despite several of the soldiers coming from north of the Arctic Circle they all found life in the Moray climate very unpleasant.

Under the control of Scottish Command, the Norwegians, in 1941, were ordered on their great festival day, the 17th of May, to entrain for Tain, 'theirs not to reason why.' In Tain, the Royal Hotel was much frequented and it was there that King Haakon, with Prince Olaf, stayed when he came to inspect the Norwegian Brigade. However, their stay at Tain was not to be for long and in the autumn of 1941 the Norwegians were sent to Banff where they were employed on the very unpopular task of erecting anti-aircraft defences on the neighbouring beaches.

The next winter of 1941/42 was even harder than the previous one and the Norwegians, though grateful to the Scots for asylum were somewhat caustic about the level of winter proofing of homes and other buildings and the general inadequacy of the methods of heating. Many Norwegians trained in the Cairngorms and after being served 'two eggs on my plate' disappeared, either by aircraft or 'tonk tonk' back to their native land.

In Banff the Brigade was attached to the 51st Division, but was subsequently transferred to the 52nd and shifted from Tain to Dingwall where they occupied Brahan Castle. Not long after their arrival at Brahan the Norwegian Brigade was posted to England and away from greater Moray, leaving behind their fishing fleet and secret service compatriots.

Adjacent to Moray and often exercising in Moray was a training camp of The Kompani Linge. This clandestine unit had been established in 1940, by Captain Martin Linge of the Norwegian Army, with its headquarters at Glenmore Lodge. There, in seclusion and in terrain similar to Norway the Kompani Linge rehearsed various operations against the Germans, including landing on the Lofoten Islands on Christmas Day 1941. Captain Linge was killed on a similar audacious operation a day or two later. But the Kompani continued and carried out the successful raid on the heavy water plant at Vermork. They also went through the motions of blowing up the railway viaduct over the Findhorn at Tomatin.

In 1973 the local community erected a stone to the memory of Kompani Linge and the inscription reads:

> 'This stone was erected by the people of Badenoch in honour of the gallant Company of Norwegian patriots who lived among them and trained in these mountains, 1941-45, to prepare for operations in occupied Norway. By skilful and daring raids on military and industrial targets they harassed the enemy and denied him vital supplies. These dangerous missions were not carried out without losses. 57 brave men of Kompani Linge gave their lives in our common cause.'

The Americans

Despite the sour grapes popular saying 'The Yanks are over paid, over sexed and over here' they were far and away the most popular foreign troops, primarily because they spoke a form of English and were considerably better paid than their British equivalent. The first GI's (Government Issue) were engineers who arrived in Moray in the spring of 1942 and started to lay concrete runways at Kinloss and Lossiemouth. They brought with them the latest in heavy earth moving plant and equipment and honed the skills that they would use in building airfields on the Pacific islands where their speed of airfield construction astonished and dismayed the Japanese, as within days of capturing an island the American heavy bombers took off to pound Japanese cities. It is perhaps not fully appreciated in this country that Tokyo was almost completely destroyed by island based bombers months before the nuclear explosions at Hiroshima and Nagasaki.

The Yanks, as they were popularly called, though this went down like the proverbial lead balloon with those who hailed from south of the Mason-Dixon line, were not stationed in any numbers in Moray, though there were some visitors from the U.S.Air Force (originally part of the Army Air Force) and the occasional GI on leave trying to find his roots or relatives. By the spring of 1944 practically all the American soldiers had drained away to the south of England in preparation for their part in OVERLORD, the invasion of Europe.

The Canadian Forestry Corps

Every soldier requires four full-grown trees to support him. His share of a mess room, table and chair needs the timber from one tree. A second tree provides boxes to carry ammunition etc while the third tree is used in making the stock for his rifle and duck boards to walk on while the fourth supplies wood for aircraft, and shipping.

The war demanded an increased supply of timber, but in 1939 Britain was the largest wood importing country in the world and shipping was urgently required for food and munitions. Home grown timber, unsatisfactory as it might be, would have to fill the gap but, unfortunately, there were not enough experienced forestry workers to fell and prepare the large amounts of timber required.

Despite the use of secondary school children, skilled labour with adequate machinery was what was required and as early as 1939 forestry workers were being recruited in Newfoundland. At that time, Newfoundland was not part of Canada and the workers were civilians and were designated as the Newfoundland Forest Unit. One such worker was the late Mr. Hawco, founder of the automobile business in Elgin, which bears his name. There were also volunteers from Australia and New Zealand and a 500 strong band from Honduras who were sent, inadequately prepared to work in a Scottish winter.

However it was Canada which provided the majority of the timber workers, and trained the men as soldiers first and then workers, so that the men could pick up their rifles if required. By mid 1941 almost 7,000 were employed at 33 camps, of which two were on the Darnaway estate, one at Darnaway itself and the other at Cooperhill. There was a clutch of camps round Cawdor and several more in upper Strathspey while timber was being worked on most estates in Moray at that time.

The Canadians introduced mechanisation into the production of timber, providing electric generators, diggers, bulldozers and the widespread use of circular saws. When foot and mouth disease broke out on 2nd January 1942 at Tain it was Canadian machinery which dug the trenches for the incineration of the slaughtered animals.

Socially, the Canadians integrated well with the locals. Several of the incomers' ancestors had emigrated within living memory and many cousins were united. Marriages, perhaps a few bigamous, were popular and at Carbridge Camp it was noted that there was a marriage a month between a Canadian lad and a local lass. At Christmas the Canadians entertained the local children, while at Cawdor they entertained themselves with a barrel of fine malt which they managed to abstract from Royal Brackla distillery. A little fracas in Forres resulted in a shop door being damaged. The owner was quite prepared to accept this as natural in war time and was most surprised and delighted to receive compensation from the Canadian Army.

The close connections between Canada and Scotland, renewed during the War, were, for many years, kept alive by Scottish Canadian Associations, such as existed in Inverness and Elgin. But the passage of time and the death of the first generation has diminished the need for such organisations and now only a few old men and women remember with affection these lumbermen soldiers with the "Canada" flash on their shoulder and the ready smile on their lips.

The Indians

The Indians are a bit of a mystery. These were Indians from the Empire. Fine upstanding men with a martial tradition and black flowing beards, but how or why they were in Moray is not now known. What is known is that they appeared in Moray in 1940 and were in tents in the grounds of Gordon Castle. They were believed to be a mountain artillery company using mules to carry the guns and ammunition while the officers and senior NCOs rode magnificent chargers.

After leaving Gordon Castle they moved to Cluny Hill at Forres and later they moved to a tented encampment at Loch Insh in Badenoch. Seton Gordon writes, 'During the war Indian troops were encamped beside Loch Insh; one met them, galloping furiously on horseback...their black beards streaming in the wind.' The Indians were liked by the natives, for their manners were exemplary, and no doubt they felt at home in a hill country. As considerate in their departure as in their stay, they left quietly and unobtrusively.

The Airmen

In politically correct circles it is now considered distinctly 'non U' to speak of the Empire. But the young men and women who left the safety of their homes in the outback of Australia, the veldt of Africa, the farms of Rhodesia, the prairies of Canada and the colonies of the Carribean and East and West Africa were proud to serve the Empire and even prouder, to wear as a shoulder flash, the particular country to which they belonged. The ones who came to Moray were mainly in the Air Force, sometimes as members of complete squadrons and occasionally as individuals. Even now, after sixty years, it is still heartbreaking to look at the grave-stones at the military cemeteries of Kinloss and Lossiemouth and in Bellie Kirkyard see the names and ages of the young men, boys in fact, who came from all over the Empire to die for an ideal which would not last much longer than their own brief lives.

Dallachy was almost certainly more clearly representative of Empire than any other airfield in Britain. The anti-shipping Strike Wing assembled there in October 1944 consisted of 144 Squadron RAF, 404 RCAF, 455 RAAF, 489 RNZAF. These four Beaufighter squadrons contributed equally to the 2235 sorties flown from this airfield into enemy waters. At this stage in the war the Wing's mass attack methods had driven shipping from the Norwegian coastal waters and normal berths to hide by day in the fiords, the narrower the better, This made mass attack impossible and the aircraft were forced to attack in file in pairs, a method often effective but difficult and dangerous, as flanking fire came from the shores as well as from the ships.

On 7th February, the German destroyer Z-33 was en route to Bergen from Trondheim, but after grounding it was decided to return to Trondheim for examination and repairs. Early on the morning of the 9th February, Z-33 entered Fördefjord and anchored near the entrance. Later that morning two Beaufighters from the New Zealand 489 Squadron spotted the destroyer and several other ships before returning to Dallachy for a late lunch. As the crew of the reconnaissance Beaufighters ate the customary bacon and eggs, the rest of the station was engaged in refuelling and rearming almost every available and serviceable aircraft while scrambled telephone calls were being made to the Admiralty and, most importantly, to RAF Peterhead arranging for Mustang fighter cover.

By 14.00 the strike force of thirty-one Beaufighters was in the air closely followed by two Warwicks which were to act as air-sea rescue aircraft. Over the Scottish coast they picked up their escort of twelve Mustangs from Peterhead; this total force of forty five aircraft being under the command of Wing Commander Colin Milsom, an Australian and his somewhat ancient navigator, thirty-five year old Flying Officer Ralph E. Jones. Shortly after clearing the Scottish coast one of the Mustangs developed engine trouble and returned to base escorted by another Mustang. The depleted but still impressive strike force continued north-eastwards.

At this stage in the war the strike force had developed a very effective method of attack on enemy shipping in the Norwegian fjords. The procedure was to use the mountains to hide their approach and to suddenly appear up the fjord but heading west towards the target and the open sea. With luck the aircraft could strafe the target with rockets and cannon fire and would be well on its way home before the luckless ship's crew could respond. This was the plan which Wing Commander Milsom expected to put into operation as his force approached Fördefjord from the south and about a third of the way up the fjord.

As his aircraft came over the lip of the mountains and over the water, intending to turn west and fly over the target ships, to his surprise German flak ships as well as the guns of the destroyer Z-33 opened up underneath his unprepared crew. In the interval between the reconnaissance and the attack the Germans had moved their ships into a better defensive position. With no room to manoeuvre Milsom turned to the right and flew up the fjord where he regrouped his force over Förde and led them once more on a steep but manageable attack path.

The flight up the fjord and the regrouping had taken up valuable time and twelve Focke-Wulf 190s were scrambled from Herdla at Bergen and were on their way to do battle. This was a substantial number of the few Luftwaffe fighters still serviceable in Norway and it was led by two experienced pilots, Feldwebel (Sergeant) Rudolf Artner and Leutnant (Lieutenant) Rudolf Linz. Milsom and Jones made the first attack on the enemy ships, coming down over the mountains and blasting their targets with rockets and automatic fire before turning down the fjord and racing out to sea and safety. Following them were other Beaufighters including one of 144 Squadron RAF, piloted by Pilot Officer Smith with Pilot Officer Holly as his navigator. These two were on their last operation and that is exactly what it was, as a Focke-Wulf chased them up the valley at Naustdal and out to sea where the two RAF men crashed and were taken prisoner. They had the doubtful distinction of being the first Beaufighter to be shot down that day

Over twenty-five years later, in 1978 Spike' Holly's seat was dredged up from Høydais fjord and can now be seen at the small, but excellent, museum at Fochabers.

Aircraft EE-V of 404 Squadron, piloted by Pilot Officer Blunderfield, was the second casualty. William Edward Blunderfield, aged 22 at the time of his death, lies at Haugesund, far from his native Toronto while his navigator Pilot Officer William James Jackson has no known grave. Amongst others to die that day were Flying Officer O.W.Knight who would not

Fig 28. Holly's seat
Photo: Courtesy Alex Fraser

return to his Doreen at Vancouver nor would Hugh Charles Lynch, his navigator, see Ottawa again.

In total, nine Beaufighters and one Mustang were shot down but many of the Beaufighters which survived to limp back to Dallachy had to be written off. The Germans lost four of their aircraft and two of their pilots, including one of their top 'aces', Leutnant Rudolf Linz who was almost casually shot down by a short burst of fire from a Beaufighter which appeared underneath his aircraft. At the age of 28, Linz had been credited with 70 kills.

The results of the attack were disappointing. Although it was claimed that a destroyer was sunk, Z-33 continued on its way to Trondheim. Several sailors were killed and many more wounded, both on the destroyer and accompanying vessels, but the RAF never again attacked surface vessels of the Kriegsmarine, switching its attention to transport ships and especially submarines.

Fig 29. Dallachy Strike Wing memorial
Photo: A.B. Loveland

But the comradeship shown by these sons of the Empire who gave of their youth is still something of a legend in Moray to this day. Each year there is a ceremony at Dallachy where old men remember and, though the inscription below is on a granite block thousands of miles away, the words are as relevant today as when carved, two generations ago:

' When you go home,

tell them of us, and say,

for your tomorrow

we gave our today '

(A British War Memorial
inscription - Kohima, India)

WORLD WAR II
IN MORAY

PART SIX

MILITARY
ADMINISTRATION

Part Six
Military Administration

Camps and Accommodation

The influx of troops into Moray at the outbreak of the war and their subsequent movement to and fro during the war years created a demand for accommodation for a variety of purposes such as storage, training and living both for our own troops and allies and also for prisoners of war. Empty properties were quickly requisitioned and the shortfall was made up by the rapid construction of hutted camps sited throughout the district.

The closure of most of the distilleries consequent on the diversion of raw materials for food consumption made these establishments available for billeting troops The malt barns and outbuildings along with Manager's, Cooper's and Excise houses were also pressed into service. Elsewhere purpose built camps were constructed mainly for training the new intake of volunteers and conscripts. Chief among these camps was one on the eastern outskirts of Elgin at Pinefield, now an Industrial Estate.

Fig 30. The Guardroom at Pinefield Camp today.
Photo: W A B

The camp was built in 1938, in anticipation of the outbreak of war, on Linkwood ground and consisted of prefabricated wooden huts supplied by F D Cowieson of Glasgow, a firm specialising in the supply and erection of portable buildings in the UK and the colonies. Most of the huts were later clad in brickwork in the 1950s by the firm of 'Tarmac Ltd.'

The camp in the early days of the war, 1939-43, housed The Royal Engineers and RE OCTU cadets under training. Basic infantry training was carried out at the camp and training in military field-works was carried out at what was called the 'upper field-works ground' at Woodside on the north east side of Elgin where there was scope for instruction in trench and dug-out construction, and the techniques of barbed wire defences, mines, minefields, demolitions and explosives including grenades, all traditional 'Sapper' work very much in the mould of first world war teaching. The rifle range was on the adjacent ground where the refuse dump is now.

Fig 31. One of the original wooden huts to which
brick cladding was not added.
Photos W A B

'Bailey' and pontoon bridging was taught and practised on the estuary at Findhorn where there was a site incorporating a large store and launching ramp. The store survives and now houses the Findhorn Boatyard business. The training staff were accommodated in Nissen huts at the boatyard whilst the trainees were housed in Nissen huts in a camp at Pineridge near where the Findhorn Foundation later set up their establishment.

Fig 32. Training Staff hut
Photo: W A B

Fig 33. The former wet-
bridging store.
Photo: W A B

Fig 34. Pontoon bridging -
Winter 1940.
Photo: W A B

Apart from the weather the main problem in training at Findhorn was the rapid
tides that ebbed and flowed into and out of the bay, which made handling the
ungainly pontoon equipment exceedingly testing for the untrained troops.
Fortunately there was a powerful RE Motor Boat on stand-by to rescue any
units that looked like being swept out to sea.

Fig 35. A pontoon raft under oars.
Photo: W A B

'Small Box Girder' bridging training was carried out at Gilston Loch, north of Elgin, NGR NJ 205661, now infilled with the concrete from abandoned airfields. Here recruits were also taught how to cross a water obstacle without boats, rafts or bridges. The technique was to strip and bundle the clothing in the waterproof gas cape and swim across the obstacle with the rifle or sten gun balanced on top of the bundle which was pushed along in front of the swimmer. This exercise went on even during the winter months. A car-breaking firm now occupies the store building where the bridging equipment was maintained.

Fig 36. A small box girder bridge mounted on a Mark II
Churchill tank ready for placing in position for an assault.
Photo: Courtesy Bovington Tank Museum

At the start of the war Infantry Depots were expanded to form Infantry Training Centres. No.11 Seaforth and Cameron ITC was removed from Fort George in 1943 to Pinefield Camp when the Fort George barracks and training area was required for practice for the D-day landings of operation OVERLORD. The Churchill tanks and their crews of 5 Assault Regiment RE were accommodated here during the winter of 1942/3.

Fig 37. A Churchill tank, Armoured Vehicle R E (AVRE).
Photo: Courtesy Bovington Tank Museum

It was from the shores beneath the walls of the Fort that the tanks went aboard the Tank Landing Craft (LCTs) for weekly exercises at sea and practice assault landings on the Culbin Sands.

Fig 38. Tanks and crews of 5 ARE and RM Commandos embarked on LCTs at Terneuzen for the battle of the Scheldt. Note the ships are survivors of D Day and still carry the 3 Div badge, the vehicles carry the 79 Armd Div badge (see also Appendix 3)
Photo: W A B

By far the greatest amount of accommodation specially constructed for use during the war was concentrated around the numerous airfields that sprang up on the flat lands of the Laich of Moray. These are dealt with in some detail in Part Three. Most of these camps have now been demolished along with the other airfield installations including the runways, but the occasional hut can still be found either derelict or converted to agricultural use. The remains of a few brick-built huts can still be seen on the edge of former Balnageith airfield near Forres, for example. Some of these were used later in the war to house PoWs.

Prisoners of War

Apart from our own troops the area saw some of the Allies, and units of the Indian Army were stationed for a time at Gordon Castle Fochabers and there were Polish troops stationed at Dallachy. As the war progressed the safeguarding and accommodation of Prisoners of War became a problem starting even in 1939.

The eventual overcrowding was relieved when the US agreed to take some PoWs and they were shipped to camps in Texas and elsewhere in the US and in Canada. PoW camps were established throughout the country. The camps housed as prisoners, men taken in combat who had been fighting either in the Italian or German armies.

They were not all necessarily of Italian or German nationality. Occasionally they were men who had been pressed into serving their dictatorial masters.

The majority of these PoW camps were concentrated in England in the midlands and the southern counties. There were far fewer in Wales and in Scotland. Morayshire had three camps located at Craigellachie; another one was near the farm of Auchness at NGR NJ 116 490 two miles south of Dallas, and another was at Logie near the former Dunphail railway station.

Camp No. 67 at Craigellachie, AKA Archiestown, was situated near Sandyhillock NGR NJ56 449. The Commandant was Major Murray-Lyon. In 1945 it is recorded as housing an Italian Labour Battalion. (PRO FO 939/148) The camp appears to have had various out-stations or 'hostels'. One of these was in a hutted camp at Nethybridge, opened in August 1945, where there were German prisoners returned from the USA. Another hostel was at Cairnfield House, Buckie, opened in September 1945. This camp was in a mansion house and also housed Germans from the USA. At this time, 1945, the war was over in Europe and PoW's were being returned, for repatriation, to the UK from the USA where they had been in camps in Texas. There was also a camp or 'hostel' at Fochabers and a hostel near Dallas at Craigroy Farm NGR NJ 120501. The farmer was James Shaw and transport was provided by A Falconer and Sons, Elgin.

Fig 39. The remains of the PoW camp at Moss Side
near Logie. The camp is said to have housed about
100 Italian Pows. They were employed In the nearby
Logie and Dunphail Estate's woodlands.
Photo: W A B

At Findhorn the camp or hostel was beside Culleme Farm and there was a playing field adjacent where John Whyte of Findhorn remembers playing football against a team of German PoWs. There seem to have been several camps or hostels at Forres based originally on Balnaferry House and including part of Balnageith airfield at a later date. There was a hostel at Ladybridge and a camp at Logie near the farm of Moss Side at NGR NJ 022500.

During the war most of these camps were guarded with barbed wire patrolled by sentries. After the cessation of hostilities security was greatly relaxed whilst prisoners waiting for repatriation were allowed out to work. In Morayshire this work was mainly on the farms and prisoners were permitted to wear civilian clothes or to wear their issue uniforms with the coloured aiming patches removed, most of them retained their own military headresses throughout their captivity. The issue uniform for PoWs was ordinary British battledress dyed chocolate brown and with large brightly coloured patches, aiming marks, sewn onto the back, front over the heart and one leg. Being allowed out to work generated a widespread and vociferous demand from the prisoners for classes in English. On the cessation of hostilities, or in the case of the Italians, when they surrendered and overnight became co-belligerents, the prisoners were given the option of repatriation or naturalisation. Despite the rules about non-fraternisation some prisoners formed friendships with local women strong enough in some cases to lead to a request for naturalisation and marriage. As most of these men were hard workers they were welcomed in a country that had suffered the attrition of its workforce as a result of battlefield casualties.

Fig 40. German PoWs in captivity marching to Germany from North Holland via the dam (Afsluitdijk) over the Ijsselmeer.
Photo: W A B

The records are most secretive about the existence of a very top secret camp situated to the east of Dallachy airfield. At this well guarded site, Germans in German uniforms and speaking only German and eating German food were preparing for return to Germany, there to cause confusion in the latter stages of the war. Three independent informants have been able to give verbal evidence of this camp but no documents have been forthcoming but rumours persist. The Public Record Office has been helpful but has no knowledge, while the Ministry of Defence has not been so helpful. All SOE records were allegedly destroyed at the end of the war and sadly nobody in Germany appears to have survived to offer his memoirs of the camp.

WORLD WAR II
IN MORAY

PART SEVEN
Ag and Fish

Part Seven

Ag and Fish

Fishing

Before the war, fishing and farming were the mainstays of the Moray economy; but when the war started they were treated very differently by the authorities. The fishermen were expected to give up boats and men while farmers were showered with money and declared to be in a reserved occupation and therefore immune from the call-up.

All along the southern coast of the Moray Firth, from Fraserbugh in the east to Inverness in the west, lie a whole string of what were once prosperous fishing villages. When boats were small they could easily enter harbours such as Hopeman and Cummingstown but over the years the move to larger boats has resulted in many of the smaller harbours crumbling into disuse and a concentration of fewer but larger boats operating from Fraserburgh, Peterhead and Aberdeen.

However, during the two world wars, the smaller harbours still serviced a few fishing boats and the more modern ones were requisitioned by the Admiralty to serve as minesweepers and supply boats. The older boats were allowed to continue fishing but had to restrict themselves to in-shore waters and be back in port by sunset when the blockade ships closed the harbour mouth. Lossiemouth can be taken as a typical example when, despite the restrictions on time spent at sea, some thirty fishermen were killed and several on naval service were decorated. The names of the dead and of their boats are immortalised in the beautiful Memorial Room of the Lossiemouth Fisherman's Museum.

Fish was never rationed, but being off the ration did not necessarily mean that it was available. The popular fish such as haddock and cod were supplemented by the greyer fleshed ling and saithe which, while never popular, were accepted thankfully and not treated with the disdain and derision which greeted the attempted introduction of snoek and whale meat into the diet in the lean post-war years.

Farming

'The Fermers are aye greetin' was a familiar comment pre-war and one that was not completely unjustified. Cheap food imports from abroad had reduced the profitability of farming and while farmers may have managed just to scrape by, the conditions of their workers was, in general, absolutely abominable. Earth floors with a single cold tap outside were commonplace for a worker's family and no amount of free meal and milk was a substitute for a living wage. There were still feeing marts at Forres and Elgin where, twice a year, workers milled about, like beasts in a pen, hoping to be offered employment by a better employer than their existing one. Work on the farm was hard and, except for the threshing, completely un-mechanised. A few farms had invested in tractors but the majority still used Clydesdales as their main motive power, resulting in ploughmen having a most peculiar gait as they followed the plough with one foot in the furrow and the other foot on the ridge. During the war and faced with the need to grow more food, the Government took an intense interest in farming and encouraged the change over from horses to tractors.

A few tractors had been used on farms since the World War I years but the depression of the early thirties prevented more than a few farmers from investing in a Ferguson or Fordson tractor. Even before World War II started the Government offered farmers £2 an acre (0.4 hectare) for ploughing up grassland and moorland pasture. Milk and meat production fell but grain and potato production rose. An acre of land used for milk or beef can support about two people, but planted in grain feeds twenty and in potatoes feeds forty.

Local Agricultural Executive Committees, composed of the good and the great farmers encouraged their neighbours in the best practices and had the power to evict any farmer deemed not to be working efficiently. Germans and Italians, the latter initially prisoners, and laterally co-belligerents, helped on the land as well as, nationally, some 90,000 Land Army girls. But, despite money being thrown at the farmers, 'the fermers are aye greetin', and at a meeting of the local National Farmers' Union in Forres in March 1941, James M'Connachie of Brodie referred to the Women's Land Army as the Women's Land Orphans and he demanded that they be organised as part of the Regular Army under army discipline. He generously conceded that such a service would not be free, but be paid for at reasonable rates.

The war ended in 1945 with most farmers in Moray in possession of at least one tractor and a considerable bank balance. Added to this was the bonus that many farmer's children were exempt from the call-up and it would appear that, on balance, farming and farmers in Moray did well out of the war.

The Women's Land Army

There had been a Women's Land Army during WW1 but despite propaganda it had not been a great success and the authorities were determined that in WW II it would be more effective. Immediately war was declared advertisements appeared in newspapers appealing to young women to join the Women's Land Army. Recruitment was initially slow but was accelerated when direction of women to war work was introduced in 1941. Many women, particularly in rural Scotland, preferred to be directed to work on the land rather than being directed to work in a factory in England.

Uniform consisted of khaki breeches, which went well with the green pullover and short great coat. There was a pert hat with a wheatsheaf badge and heavy woollen stockings and sturdy shoes completed the outfit.

Fig 41. W L A recruiting poster
HMSO

(As a small aside, WLA stockings are now on sale at £26 per pair.) For work they were supplied with overalls and, if lucky, oilskins and a sou'wester. Wages were according to age but the average was about £1.10 - £1.50 a week and there was one week's paid holiday a year. Any further time off was unpaid. If hutting or accommodation was supplied then this was deducted from their wages.

It was sometimes a lonely life and occasionally somewhat dangerous as one informant said 'Some of the farmers could be gey coorse'. But there were good times too and many a farmer's wife adopted the Land Army girl as a daughter and asked her to share meals and in the evenings sit at the fire.

But, basically the work was very hard and miserably paid with long hours and inadequate holidays but as another informant said 'it was better than going south to the factories.'

Women's Timber Corps

The war time demand for timber was insatiable and in May 1942 the Women's Timber Corps was founded in Scotland. This was a daughter to the WLA but she soon went her own way.

The uniform was similar, but the round hat was swopped for a green beret with a spruce tree badge. Welly boots replaced the wool stockings and shoes.

At this stage in the war, women were being directed into factories and even taking over from men at coal pit head jobs. This was not popular, but gruff Ernie Bevin growled that it was better to put up with temporary inconvenience than to allow the Nazis to win. Faced with working at the pits or working in the forests several girls volunteered for the Women's Timber Corps.

In the story of the Corps in Moray, the key name is not that of a lady but of Bob Allison. Bob was serving with the Argyll and Sutherland Highlanders when he was discharged from the army and placed in charge of training of applicants who wished to become foresters. There was no time for gentle introduction and as one trainee notes, "Mr. Allison was a very strict chief instructor who was determined to turn out WTC members fit to be posted anywhere in Scotland." The training camp was at Meiklour in Perthshire but after training the girls were posted to where trees were to be felled. As the late Bonny Macadam wrote, "It was a very tough life: wearing hard, leather boots, swinging heavy axes and living in stark army huts. Breakfast was at 7 o'clock: porridge, bread, margarine and tinned pilchards in tomato sauce, which I have never eaten since!" An unknown 16 years old lumberjill describes the camp at Advie, Morayshire "Forty of us shared two long wooden huts…it was rugged, draughty and most uncomfortable…We worked in all kinds of weather…wielding a six-pound axe…My quota was about sixty trees a day, five and a half days a week"

One young lady forester found both hard work and romance in Moray. Margaret Breingan was nineteen years old when she was driving a caterpillar tractor at Advie and Cromdale, and it was in Strathspey that she met her marine husband Alexander Fraser and after marriage set up home in Nethybridge. And what of Bob Allison? After training thousands of women during the war he returned to the Forestry Commission and retired to Fochabers. Few people knew that he was such a key person that he had been released from the forces in order to pass on his skill and knowledge to the women and girls of the WTC. With Bob's help and after training these girls could swing an axe and use a cross-cut saw as competently as any man.

**WORLD WAR II
IN MORAY**

PART EIGHT

MEDICAL

Part Eight

Medical

Until the National Health Service was established in 1948 there was no 'free' health care, although there was a limited scheme whereby employed people were on a 'panel' and could receive the attention of a doctor by virtue of paying for an insurance health stamp each week. Families and the non- employed were not covered and could only attend a doctor on payment of a fee, though it was practically universal that doctors charged a reduced or even no fee to the poor.

At the start of the war, all the younger doctors were called up and at Lossiemouth this left two doctors, Drs. Brander and Clark. Dr.Tom Brander was 71 years old in 1939 but Dr.Clark was too frail for night work so every time the siren went for the air raid alarm it was Dr. Brander who had to get out of bed and make his way to the first aid post. One night he was at his post when the bombs fell which killed the refugee family from Plymouth and severely damaged his own house, the ceiling coming down, but his wife was fortunately saved by being under the blankets. The damage was so extensive that the Branders had to move to the empty house of their cousins, the Levacks, who at the time were interned by the Germans in France.

In Elgin there were several medical practices. The mobilization of the Territorial Army took away one senior doctor, Alistair C.MacDonald. A.C. as he was affectionately called, later commanded an Army General Hospital in the besieged and battered island of Malta G.C. Dr. George Esson was the next to go and by 1941 Drs. Gordon Thow and Gordon Scott were the only trained and experienced surgically trained doctors left in Elgin. With most of the male doctors away at the war the arrival of female graduates from Aberdeen was generally welcomed though one or two curmudgeons, of both sexes, grumbled that they did not like being examined by a lassie. There were two doctors who lived at the top of Duff Avenue and who operated in association with Dr. Thow. These were Drs. Marie Anderson, and Helen Harkins, now Dr. Helen Gammie. A third lady assistant, Dr. Peggy Erskine, lived elsewhere. Dr. Mora Craig was assistant to Dr. Gordon Scott but it was as his wife that she was at his side in the operating theatre of Dr. Gray's on the evening of Black Friday, 9th February 1945.

Elgin was fortunate in having an hospital, erected by money left by an eccentric East Indian Company's doctor who died in the early years of the 19th century. This was a charitable organization, which charged fees for its services and employed an almoner to assess the patient's ability to pay. In 1939 the

Burgh of Elgin collected over £4,000 for the hospital and the Elgin Golf Club chipped in £7.17/- (£7.85) while the employees of Johnston's mill contributed over £4. Forres too was fortunate in having a hospital at Leanchoil which had been initially opened in 1892 and had been built with a donation of over £8,000 from Sir Donald Smith, a native of Forres, and later to be Lord Strathcona and Mount Royal.

Nurses and nursing

Warfare, as it developed in the 18th century, following upon the murderous civil conflicts of the previous century, became more 'civilised' with codes of gentlemanly conduct and a general acceptance that civilian populations, and particularly women and children, should not be wantonly destroyed. Ladies would turn out in carriages to watch the battle and no doubt a few helped the wounded, but in general, men fought and women wept.

This was the accepted state of affairs until the mid 19th century when the sufferings of the British wounded in the Crimea were brought to the attention of the public by the new steam driven presses of *The Times*, and a society lady, Florence Nightingale, along with her acolytes, sailed for Scutari to assist in nursing the sick and wounded. Nightingale was the lady with the lamp and started a legend and mightily encouraged the practice of nursing in Britain. Women had always nursed, that came with the job description, but Florence put it on a practical footing. She herself had trained at the prestigious institute at Kaiserswerth in Germany while, in 1840, Mrs. Fry had established a similar nursing centre in London where the nurses were trained at Guy's and St.Thomas' Hospitals.

On her return to Britain from the Crimea, a grateful public subscribed money to establish in 1860 the Nightingale Fund Training School for Nurses at St.Thomas' Hospital and from then on, nursing became a noble profession and ceased to be the last refuge of a gin-soaked harridan. However Florence was not the only pioneer in nursing. Ethel Gordon Manson, born in Elgin in 1857, became Matron of St Bartholomew's Hospital in London and as Mrs Ethel Bedford Fenwick established the International Congress of Nurses and became the first State Registered Nurse. She survived two world wars to die aged 90 in London. The Army, ever reluctant to have anything officially to do with women, did not establish an army nursing service until 1881 and following the experience in South Africa the Queen Alexandra's Imperial Military Nursing Service (QAIMNS) was established.

In 1914 the service was 300 strong but by 1919, the service, including reserves, amounted to 10,404. At the start of WWII there were 624 QAIMNS of whom

14 remained behind at Hong Kong. All were raped and some were murdered. These highly trained ladies, most of whom were commissioned, were helped by non-commissioned orderlies and dressers and by the Red Cross volunteers. An Elgin nurse, C.M.Arnold, working in London was killed in an air raid in October 1940.

Fig 42. The Scottish Red Cross final parade.
Courtesy of The Scotsman

The final march-past of the Scottish Branch of the British Red Cross Society before HM The Queen at Holyrood on 18 June 1946 to the tune 'Blue Bonnets over the Border' played by the Edinburgh City Pipe Band. The nurses had served in Belgium, Burma, Ceylon, France, Gibraltar, Holland, Italy and in the London Blitz as well as at the Belsen extermination camp in Germany. 180 Certificates for Distinguished War Service were awarded.

The Red Cross for the relief of suffering was founded by the Swiss banker Jean Henri Dunant who was so moved by the plight of the wounded at the battle of Solferino in June 1859 that he urged the formation of a permanent society dedicated to the relief of suffering wherever it occurred. War time volunteers were trained in first aid and elementary nursing, but could, on occasion, find themselves called upon to undertake duties far beyond their remit, but still expected to be carried out. At the start of the war there were 400 trained Voluntary Aid Detachment (VAD) personnel in Moray The president of the Morayshire branch of the Red Cross was Barbara, Countess of Moray and the war had barely started when she was appealing for funds. This was to be a constant refrain throughout the war as the demands placed upon the organization increased greatly during the years. The first initial appeal raised £81, but subsequent appeals gathered in much more. As British soldiers were taken prisoner so the demands on the Red Cross became heavier but it never became a bureaucratic organization and, when in 1944 hundreds of starving enemy prisoners were decanted at Forres it was the Red Cross which initiated order into the chaos and made arrangements for the starving men to be fed.

First Aid Nursing Yeomanry (F.A.N.Y.)

This was one of the oddest yet effective voluntary bodies of two world wars. It had its genesis in the Boer War when the virtues of having a mounted nurse who could rapidly reach a wounded man and give first aid was recognised. It was also intended that this angel of mercy would be armed so that she could skirmish with the regular cavalry if required. The idea was advanced by Kitchener and by 1907 the first F.A.N.Y.s were enrolled. Despite wearing uniform, these were civilians and initially had to pay for the honour of being enlisted. This ensured that only girls of a privileged background could become members. With privilege came education and while most were content to drive ambulances and staff cars, during WW II many entered the intelligence services and 2,000 became members of the Special Operations Executive (S.O.E.). Of these, 13 were murdered by the Gestapo, some by lethal injection and the others by a bullet in the back of the neck. At the time, FANYs were the only female personnel authorised to carry firearms. There is a Moray born lady still living in Elgin now who served in the FANYs.

Ambulances

Elgin had two ambulances, operated by the St.Andrew's Ambulance Association. This again was a charitable organization which was founded in Glasgow in 1881 and gave training in first aid and supplied stretchers and wheeled litters, the first ambulances. By 1886 the number of trained first aiders was 7,401 with ambulances stationed in Glasgow, Edinburgh, Dumbarton, Paisley, Hamilton and Bailleston. Before the turn of the century there was a branch of the Association in Elgin and after 1908 the Association co-operated closely with the Red Cross. There was also an ambulance at Forres, but this was like a horse-box or small caravan which was towed by a motor car.

WORLD WAR II
IN MORAY

PART NINE

CIVIL DEFENCE

Part Nine
Civil Defence

Air Raid Precautions

By 1939 even the most optimistic realised that war with Germany was now inevitable, but already, in 1938, discreet preparations had been taking place to prepare the civilian population for the ordeals ahead. A system of civil defence with local people to guide, give advice and, if necessary, dig people out of the rubble was set up. These local guides were known as wardens and were civilians with no ranks, though one assumed the rank and title of the Chief Warden. Initially they were equipped with the standard steel helmet and service gas mask but later in the war their army issue helmets were withdrawn and they were issued with a lighter and more conical shaped helmet while their service respirator was replaced with a heavier version of the civilian type. Each warden was also issued with a sterling silver badge and a stirrup pump.

Initially there was little practical experience to guide the people responsible for setting up an organisation to deal with the possibility of enemy air-raids. Some crazy schemes were suggested. The ARP Controller for Morayshire was F O Stuart, a Lossiemouth councillor and chairman of the Joint County Council of Moray and Nairn. At a meeting in Elgin he suggested, in answer to a question from Provost Mackay of Nairn, that 'the public would have to scatter to the hills should there be an attack from the air' (Courant 9-10-1936 5/6). Another suggestion put forward in all seriousness was to turn the town's closes into shelters by applying another layer of brick round them.(Forres Gazette 10-7-1940, 3/4).

One of the chief dangers anticipated was a poison gas attack. The Government had put out leaflets requiring people to carry their gas masks with them at all times. They also recommended that each household should prepare a gas-proof room to which people could retreat in an air raid. This was before the general issue of respirators to all members of the public

Hitler will send no warning – so always carry your gas mask

Fig 43. Gas warning poster
HMSO

129

Fortunately these rooms were never tested in anger and neither were the respirators.

Each Burgh was divided into a series of numbered sectors (See advert from the Forres Gazette 15-05-40 *sequens*) based on well known and prominent landmarks such as garages, Burgh offices etc. Each sector had a telephone and was presided over by a senior warden. All sectors were in touch with the local control centre with a chief and a deputy warden. Unless a raid was in progress the wardens patrolled their designated areas checking that the blackout regulations were being observed and taking any action necessary in case of infringement of any of the various wartime regulations that hemmed about the civilian population. The various public air-raid shelters were checked and supervised.

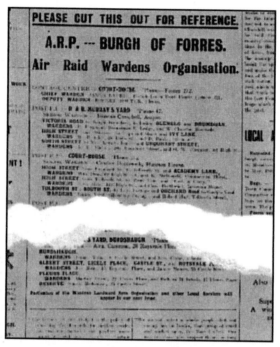

Fig 44. Part of an ARP notice
in the Forres Gazette

In the event of an air raid the wardens made sure that any citizens caught out in the open were safely escorted to the nearest shelter. They watched the progress of the raid and reported any bombs dropped and damage caused so that the controller was able to send the appropriate assistance to the scene. It was particularly important to keep a lookout for dud or delay action bombs. Fortunately the organisation was rarely tested in Morayshire and was able to deal adequately with the few incidents that did occur.

Areas designated 'unclassified' were prompted to provide public shelters in streets and locations convenient to places where people were likely to congregate. Private persons were encouraged to make their own arrangements, it being suggested that the home would probably be the safest place providing some basic precautions were taken, like minimising the likelihood of flying glass by pasting strips of paper over the windows. A reinforced form of dining table was made available beneath which the family was supposed to take shelter when a raid was imminent. This was called a Morrison shelter.

Anderson shelters, those DIY corrugated iron shelters designed to be dug partly below ground to provide shelter on a domestic scale were available to some authorities. Public buildings like hospitals were provided with adequate purpose built shelters and blast walls of sandbags.

Fig 45. An Anderson shelter after a near miss (not in Moray).
Photo: Courtesy Imperial War Museum London

Fig 46. Outside Leanchoil Hospital, Forres in 1939.
*Note: wall of sandbags, and small boy
with a gas mask hanging at his side.*
Photo: Courtesy R.R. MacKenzie

Schools were provided with slit trenches dug close to the buildings so that pupils could take shelter as quickly as possible. These trenches were zig-zag in plan and were some four feet deep by three to four feet wide with the excavated earth banked up on either side.

Auxiliary Fire Service

The growing threat of war induced the government to set up The Fire Brigades Act, 1938 (1&2 Geo.VI,c.72) which received the Royal Assent on 28 July 1938. This Act empowered 1,440 separate statutory authorities in England and Wales and 228 in Scotland, to set up a total of 1,668 Fire Brigades. Section 14(3) of the Act provided that every District council had to provide fire protection, and that every person was entitled to the services of a fire brigade without charge.

Recruiting for an Auxiliary Fire Service (AFS) began in 1938 and 30,000 auxiliary firemen and firewomen had been enrolled by April. The fire women were assigned to control and watchroom duties and to any other job within their capabilities that would release able-bodied firemen for active fire-fighting work. By September the AFS had expanded to a total of 89,000 men and 6,000 women for full time service and had been integrated with the standing fire service of about 5,000 plus a volunteer and retained service of about 50,000. This force was equipped with some 14,000 emergency trailer pumps.

In 1940 the fall of France and the occupation of the Low Countries allowed the enemy to move his airfields up to the English Channel thus placing his aircraft within range of a large part of Britain. Air raids now began with increasing frequency and intensity. The subsequent casualties created a new sense of urgency to address problems of organisation and shortages of equipment. The treasury authorised the issue of 2,000 two-ton vans as auxiliary towing equipment to replace the odd collection of vehicles that had been pressed into service at the outbreak of war. These vans were equipped with hoses and other necessary items.

Early in 1941 a further bill received the Royal Assent providing for the reorganisation and nationalisation of the fire service.(It lasted until 1947 when a further Act returned the service to local authority control). The new National fire Service (NFS) took over duties from the AFS brigades in August. The country was now organised into 33 fire areas in England and 6 in Scotland, split again into divisions of 100 pumps and crews, the number varying with the size of the force. Each division was comprised of two columns each of five companies of ten pumps and crews in each column, commanded by a column officer.

In Moray fire protection was provided by eleven retained brigades. These units were scattered around the county from Lossiemouth in the north to Tomintoul in the south and from Forres in the west to Keith in the east. The first full time fire station for the county was built in Elgin and was opened in 2001. Prior to that the retained brigade operated out of premises at Marywell during the war and until a new station was built at Haugh Road in 1953. This former station has now been demolished as a site for a new supermarket.

Fig 47. Elgin NFS at Marywell, about 1943.
Photo: D. Munro

One of the most notable conflagrations in Elgin during the war occurred in December 1939 when the Town Hall in Moray Street, now the site of the Police Station which was erected nearly twenty years later, was accidentally set on fire The Hall was being used as a billet for troops at the time and it was completely gutted despite the best efforts of the Auxiliary Fire Service. Later in the war the town's stables were also destroyed by fire with the sad loss of the heavy horses that were used for pulling the 'scaffy' carts. A certificate was eventually obtained allowing the purchase of a Bedford lorry, but the bin-men threatened to go on strike as the overtime, necessary to look after the horses, was not required for the lorry. The Burgh Surveyor had to read the riot act and point out that striking in wartime could land the striker in jail and the incipient trouble was thus avoided.

Apart from the usual incidence of fire from accidental causes there was now the very real threat of fire as a result of enemy air activity. One of the indiscriminate weapons favoured by the enemy was the widespread use of incendiary bombs, usually mixed in with a quota of high explosive bombs some of which were not infrequently delay action bombs. These were designed to go off after an interval when they would create casualties amongst the rescue services. The menace of the incendiary bomb was met by fire watching parties on principal buildings and establishments whose role was to extinguish any incendiaries dropped before they could do any real damage. To that end these parties were equipped with long handled scoops, a bucket of sand and a bucket of water with a stirrup pump. Every prudent householder was recommended also to equip himself with these items.

Women's Voluntary Service

Parallel to the male orientated ARP (Air Raid Precautions) warden service was the entirely female WVS (Women's Voluntary Service) now the WRVS. This had its genesis in the first aid and gas defence classes which Lady Reading held in her home at the start of 1938. By April of that year Lady Reading was telling the Home Secretary that a General Secretary was required to organise an expanded system of classes. The WVS was a voluntary service and there were to be no ranks and on 16 June 1938 the new body was introduced to the public. Later that year a quarter of a million women were available to voluntarily carry out official orders. In Scotland, the chairman during the critical war years was Lady Ruth Balfour.

Church of Scotland Canteens

Various different charitable and voluntary organisations provided static and mobile canteens during the war. These 'Good Samaritans' brought the comfort of tea and buns to military installations both large and small no matter how hazardous or difficult of access. The canteens followed the troops wherever they were stationed both at home and abroad. In Moray the mobile canteens were provided by the Church of Scotland. At the outbreak of war the C of S had only a small fleet of four mobile canteens but by 1940 this number had increased to a fleet of forty and with the addition of thirty six static canteens or 'Huts' as they called them. The service was provided to the Royal Navy, the Army, the Royal Air Force, the Merchant Navy, and the Women's Auxiliary services and members of the Home

Fig 48 A typical canteen scene
' Somewhere in Scotland ' 1939-1945
Photo: Courtesy Alex Fraser

Guard in uniform. The number of vans allocated to Moray is uncertain but there was at least one mobile canteen centered on Elgin and it was housed, when off duty, in a lock-up garage somewhere in the Collie Street vicinity, an area that has seen some re-development since the war so it is now no longer possible to pinpoint the exact location.

These vans were arranged with a drop-down hatch at the side or back, which formed a counter for the 'customers.' The lady volunteers had tea making facilities and stocks of 'goodies' such as cigarettes, matches, stationery and postage stamps. etc., all items in frequent demand by the troops. The shout of 'tea up' was eagerly awaited on many a dreary training area or airfield, in Moray, by soldiers and airmen alike. There was a water tank on the roof of the van and on one memorable occasion a lady, who shall be nameless, in a moment of temporary aberration tried to drive the van through the archway at Pansport with dire results to the water tank.

As the *Report of the Committee on the Hut and Canteen work for H.M. Forces* puts it, 'these cars have carried the white cross of St Andrew, often faded and dust-covered, but always welcomed, and everywhere recognised and honoured for the fine record it has so worthily established and maintained-- a record of unselfish and unflinching readiness to follow our fighting men wherever duty or danger may take them'.

WORLD WAR II
IN MORAY

PART TEN

CIVIL
ADMINISTRATION

Part Ten
Civil Administration

The Home Front

At the outbreak of war the authorities had many worries but one of the two foremost amongst them was the fear of imminent bombing, probably using poison gas, and the other was the morale of the civilian population. The first did not appear until more than nine months later, and then gas was not employed, while morale was kept up by an all pervasive censorship which suppressed as far as practicable any bad news while any good news, trivial or otherwise, was widely broadcast.

Within a few weeks of the start of the war the Ministry of Information had a staff of 1,000. Despite their numbers, or maybe because of them, it perpetuated an early gaffe by issuing a poster '**Your** Courage, **Your** Cheerfulness, **Your** Resolution Will Bring **Us** Victory.'

The Black Out

From Friday, 1st September, all street lights were switched off and no premises were allowed, under pain of punishment for the occupants, to show the slightest light. As the politically incorrect doggerel went:

> ' *Chink at the window,*
> *Jap at the door,*
> *Italy last time,*
> *Czecho no more.* '

Pedestrian navigation at night was very difficult and on a really dark night, collisions were frequent. Clear starlit nights allowed observation of the Aurora Borealis while nights with a moon were much valued for helping people to get around after dark; although, after the start of the Blitz it came to be called 'a bomber's moon' and was not so popular in certain districts, for obvious reasons.

You were allowed to use a flashlight, provided you could obtain batteries and the circle of light was not larger than 1in (2.5cm) diameter and shone through frosted glass. Motor vehicle headlamps were hooded and threw a miserable flattened beam while rear and side lamps were also dimmed. A stripe of white paint was applied round the edges of the mudguards and on the bumpers.

Despite this motor accident rates increased, the first fatal one in Moray occurred on the 2 September when William Mitchell, a foreman with a firm of contractors from Grantown-on-Spey, was killed on the road.

Later in the war civilian road casualties fell a little when the shortage of petrol reduced civilian traffic. 'Summer time' was all the year round and during the actual summer the light evenings were extended by yet another hour. A major cause of civilian casualties was people falling into the unfenced harbours. In January 1944 two wives of servicemen fell into the water at Lossiemouth. In the same week, but in an unconnected incident, two Airmen fell into the same harbour but, fortunately for both, they were rescued.

The black out, in all its strict severity, lasted until September 1944, five years in total, when it was partially lifted for a time known as 'the dim-out'. But this was of only slight benefit as few street lamps or lighting systems were able to operate. Complete restrictions on illumination, bon-fires etc. were finally abandoned with the defeat of Germany.

Rationing

In 1939 Britain imported 3.4 million tons of wheat and 1.6 million tons of sugar as well as a million tons of meat. All were carried on ships which had to run the gauntlet of enemy U-boats because the Germans knew that starvation was eventually a more decisive weapon than bombs. Strangely enough, Churchill with his experience at the Admiralty was against the early introduction of rationing and it was not until Monday, 8 January 1940 that butter, bacon and sugar became only obtainable on coupons.

The 'Northern Scot' detailed the limitations to the fairly reasonable amounts of Sugar 12 ozs (335g), Bacon 4 ozs (110g) and Butter 4 ozs (110g). All throughout the war extra sugar was available in summer for making jam and beekeepers were also given an allowance. People were also advised to register with butchers as it was intended to introduce rationing in February 1940.

In Elgin, for most of the war and into the fifties, when food rationing was eventually abolished, the office for local administration was at South Villa in Moss Street. Meat would be rationed by price; the more expensive the cut then the less weight you could buy.

To prevent any speculation it was also announced that the Ministry of Food would be the sole purchaser of all imported meat as well as of all cattle offered up for slaughter. A butt of the comedians was dried egg. This packaged food came from America and depending upon the skill of the cook could result in a passable imitation of scrambled egg or have the texture of the hide of a badly cooked camel. Then there was Spam, a minced pork and ham pressed meat that was very tasty to start with but continued exposure to it could result in revulsion. It is still available but, one suspects, little bought by the war time generation.

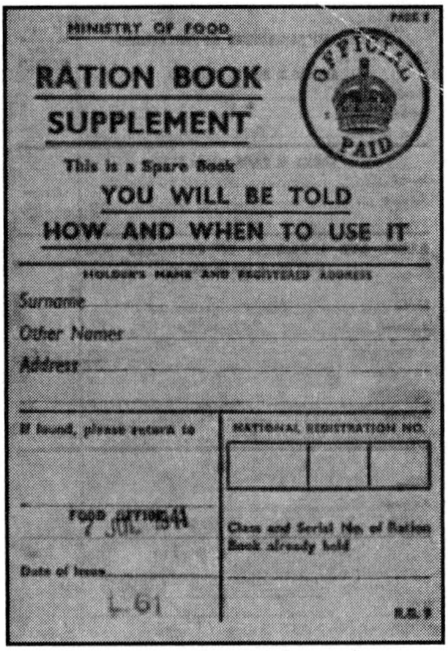
MINISTRY OF FOOD

RATION BOOK
SUPPLEMENT

OFFICIAL PAID

This is a Spare Book
YOU WILL BE TOLD
HOW AND WHEN TO USE IT

HOLDER'S NAME AND REGISTERED ADDRESS

Surname
Other Names
Address

If found, please return to

NATIONAL REGISTRATION NO.

FOOD OFFICE

Class and Serial No. of Ration Book already held

Date of Issue

L 61

Fig 49. A ration book

During the war there were no domestic freezers, few refrigerators and even fewer washing machines. A surreptitiously killed sheep, or pig had to be distributed and eaten within a few days and the recipients of this largesse would reciprocate in due course if, say, a box of fish fell off a lorry. Meat rationing was eventually introduced in March 1940 at the rate of two shillingsworth (10p) per person per week. But by July 1941 this was halved. Sufferers from pernicious anaemia were allowed an extra 1lb (650g) of liver a week, to be eaten raw!

Tea, cooking fats and margarine had been rationed from July 1940 and cheese was added to this list in 1941. Bread and potatoes were never rationed, though bread rationing was introduced after the war, and neither was coffee which at the time was considered very exotic and little drunk. Fruits, fresh or tinned, with the exception of a few oranges, were not imported and school children did not know what to do with a banana when they were eventually available.

British Restaurants, where customers could obtain plain but nourishing food, were opened in every town. The one in Elgin was opened in the disused church at the top of Moss Street. What you could spend on a meal in a conventional restaurant was also limited.

The Ministry of Information at the prompting of the Ministry of Food prepared and issued a pamphlet in 1943 containing the text of fifteen talks on the wartime diet for adults that had been broadcast by Dr. Charles Hill who was billed as 'The Radio Doctor'. The rich fruity and slightly breathless voice of the doctor had been listened to by most housewives for the latest tips to make the increasingly stringent ration go further and be more interesting and appetising.

The Minister of Food, Lord Woolton, put out many leaflets advising housewives how to make the best of the rations that were available. One of his recipes was named after him as 'Lord Woolton pie'(see Appendix 8) and the

Ministry of Food also issued a leaflet entitled 'Food Facts for the Kitchen Front' with a foreword by lord Woolton

By 1941 the harsh reality of war, or Total War as it was now being called, had reached into even the one time comfortable homes of Moray. On 1st June of that year, the President of the Board of trade announced that clothing was to be rationed from 7 June and again the 'Northern Scot' guided the public.

Every adult was to receive 66 coupons a year. A kilt was a bit of a bargain at eight coupons but if you were other than a true Scotsman it would cost you another four coupons for undergarments. Turn-ups on trousers were not allowed and later regulations prohibited the use of lace or embroidery on clothing. It was to be eight years before Harold Wilson announced in the House of Commons on 14 March 1949 that, with effect from the next day, all cloth rationing was to be abolished. Classes were held in 'make do and mend' and the late Mrs Annabella Penrose (Nan to her friends) held dressmaking sessions in New Elgin Hall.

Razor blades became very difficult to obtain and many and varied were the sharpening devices in use. Matches became rare and after the initial difficulties in obtaining flints there was a proliferation of home made cigarette lighters.

Sweets and soap were on the ration and the recently developed detergents were restricted for use in laundries with contracts for service or industrial washing Thermos flasks were obtainable by outside workers only and, if broken, could not be replaced that year. String was carefully unravelled and kept for reuse, as was brown paper and paper bags. The only china available was plain white and completely undecorated. Any complaint about availability or service was met by the inevitable response 'don't you know there's a war on?'

The Air Force, 'the brylcream boys' of Navy and Army taunts, wore separate collars with their ties and every morning, in cold dark billets throughout the land, airmen and airwomen struggled to fix their collars and tie their ties. As collar studs became unobtainable, small nuts and bolts were substituted. Until the middle of 1944 the collars, at least in the U.K. were returned, stiffly starched from the weekly laundry. As the troops landed in Normandy the order was given from the Air Ministry that forthwith no collars would be starched. The Luftwaffe must

Fig 50. A wartime poster
HMSO

have read this signal with relief; at last they were having an effect on the enemy!

It was not only food and clothing that was rationed and in short supply. Government exercised unprecedented control and influence over every aspect of civilian life. Its influence extended into the problems of shortages, even of items like furniture. This gave birth to the famous 'utility' range of products including clothing as well as furniture. Shortages of practically everything were in contrast to the manufactured goods marked for export only, earmarked as part of the effort to pay for the war. Rationing continued well into the 50s.

Evacuation

In anticipation and fear of bombing, elaborate arrangements had been made in 1938 for the evacuation of all children, including the mothers of small children, from the cities to the safety of the countryside. On September 1st 1939 these plans were put into operation and the first of millions of children were taken by special trains from the towns to the countryside.

On Moray, two trains of evacuees from Edinburgh arrived at Elgin on Saturday 2nd September and were dispersed into billets throughout the town. The WVS were literally run off their feet in arranging suitable accommodation but the centre of Elgin, with its then warren of inhabited closes, was not so different to the evacuees normal habitat and hosts and guests settled in reasonably amicably. Not so in the more rural parts of the county

By September 16th the Northern Scot headlined 'Banff's experience has been so unfortunate that practically no householder in the town will take in evacuees'. Two weeks later there was another headline, **SPEYSIDE EVACUEE TROUBLE MANY GO HOME.** The mothers of the children were blamed for the unmanageable position and the position was described as 'nothing short of fiasco'. Hints were dropped that 'a matter of cleanliness' was also involved.

It was a case of a clash of cultures. The rural hosts were generally, hard working, thrifty careful and clean people. Their guests were too often idle, and shiftless with children who did not place a high priority on washing. Added to this was the strangeness and sometimes occasional fear engendered in the new environment and the natural result in children was bed wetting at night. Many of the children had never seen a cow before and thought that milk only came in twopenny (1p) tins of Nestle condensed milk, so the sight of a large animal bellowing at them caused very real fright.

Within a few weeks most of the evacuees had returned to the cities but a few remained and forged links of friendship which lasted both time and the stresses of the long years of war.

But for the majority of both hosts and guests the experience was not the happy jolly holiday experience, which the newsreels of the time depicted. The plan to send children overseas was dropped after it was tried and the ship, the *City of Benares*, carrying them was sunk by a U-boat with the loss of 260 lives including 79 of the children.

Education was subjected to great strains and in many schools where there were evacuees, schooling became part time, with local children attending in the

Fig 51. A wartime poster
HMSO

morning and the evacuees in the afternoon. Next week the pupils changed over. At Buckie, this was the arrangement with the many Norwegian children there. University education went into top gear and an ordinary three year engineering degree was compressed into two.

There was internal evacuation in Moray and this received no publicity at the time. In the autumn of 1943 the farmers and other residents adjoining the Culbin Sands were given three weeks to vacate their farms and homes and find other accommodation for their families and livestock, as the Army and Navy wanted to carry out exercises with live ammunition on their land. The area requisitioned stretched north of a line from just north of Forres via Kintessack and including Cloddymoss to Maviston, some 6 km. east of Nairn.

The disposessed had to look around for friends and relatives who could take them in and meanwhile the grain had to be threshed and the sugar-beet had to be lifted and sent off by rail to the processing plant at Cupar in Fife. The cattle had to be sold or found temporary homes.

All this activity went on under conditions of utmost secrecy so that the majority of people in Forres and Nairn were unaware of what was happening just a few kilometres away. Immediately the inhabitants and their animals had gone, contractors moved in and widened roads and corners and after this the 'invaders' attacked and for six months the area was pounded with artillery and rockets as the 'invaders' regularly exercised for the forthcoming operation

'Overlord' wading ashore from landing craft. Several tanks are known to be lying rusting off shore and a number of servicemen lost their lives in the preparation for 'D' day.

In May 1944 a long line of tanks stretched from Forres to Burgie and as they waited to move on, local women made soup, which was much appreciated by the troops. As the soldiers moved south and on to France the dazed and almost shell-shocked evacuees were told they could return home at their own risk. Even as late as the nineteen eighties, unexploded ordnance was still being found in and around the Culbin sands. The returning evacuees found that some vandalism had taken place, but the greatest loss was the removal of all the sink plugs, which, during the war were items coveted by all troops.

In addition to the evacuation of selected categories to areas of comparative safety the Government was taking the important decision to send abroad all the gold in British banks together with the total holding of foreign securities.

On 24 June 1940 the first shipment left aboard the cruiser *HMS Emerald*. Further shipment followed in a variety of fast ships for depositing in deep vaults in Montreal. Heavily guarded all the way the entire shipment was successfully transported across the Atlantic under the unlikely codename of 'fish'.

To assist in the settlement of the huge debt, which Britain was owing to America for its help in supplying war material, Scotch Whisky was shipped across the Atlantic. One fast merchant ship, the *SS Politician*, laden with this precious cargo foundered off South Uist in the Outer Hebrides and provided the basis for Compton Mackenzie's hilarious yarn, 'Whisky Galore'.

Identity Cards

On 29th September 1939 a national census was carried out in preparation for the issue of identity cards and the control of rationing. In peacetime this would have been an extensive undertaking, but with millions of evacuees spread throughout the country and a black-out in force, the task of the enumerators was even more difficult. The card had to be carried at all times.but, lacking a photograph of the holder it was virtually useless as apositive means of identification.

The national identity card did, however, have certain beaurocratic uses proven by the fact that it was retained in use for seven years after the war ended. Also after the 18 July 1940 it should have had a slip of paper inserted giving the name and address of the next of kin.

The grey-blue folded card carried the name and unique identity number of the holder. There was no photograph and the holder had to sign the card, which had space for the owner's address and official stamps.

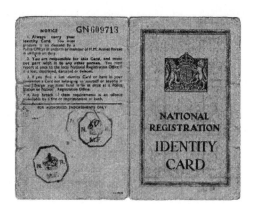

Fig 52. An ID card

Entertainment

For the maintenance of morale over the long weary years of the war entertainment was a vital factor. Although horse-racing was stopped on 19 June 1940 'until further notice,' most other forms of sport and entertainment continued. Daylight air-raids interrupted cricket but fox-hunting went on. Despite advice from landowners the government advanced the date for the start of the grouse-shooting season from the traditional twelfth to the fifth of August.

The 'wireless' was readily available at home and was a vital link with the authorities and the source of much instruction and advice. The family favourites such as Tommy Handley in ITMA, Arthur Askey and many others were looked forward to with eager anticipation. The tedium of repetitive factory production was relieved with programmes like 'Music while you work'. Dances and the Cinema were the only other forms of public entertainment in Moray. The cinema was referred to as 'the pictures' or 'the flicks' and later on as 'the movies'. Films like 'In Which We Serve' were designed to stiffen resolve as well as to entertain. From America came the music of Glen Miller and his American Army Air Force Band and 'Jitter bugging' was a popular craze on the dance floor rivalled only by 'The Lambeth Walk'.

The mood of 'here to-day and gone tomorrow' undoubtedly led to many casual liaisons, a situation exacerbated by long periods of enforced separation and statistics show that after the war there was a marked rise in the divorce rate, generally on the grounds of adultery. After closing at the start of the war London's theatres gradually reopened and the Windmill Theatre with its standard presentation of feminine nudity, a favorite for troops on leave, proudly advertised itself as 'We Never Closed'. On a higher plane the National Gallery gave Midday Concerts and Midday Ballet was available at the Arts Theatre Club for the enjoyment of those in London.

Possibly a major factor in the maintenance of morale was popular music, and it is noticeable that the popular music in Britain was markedly different from that put out over the German broadcast systems. Nazi popular music seemed always to have a direct propaganda element addressed to the German people. Based on the traditional German brass *oompah-oompah* band, the musical accompaniment to their popular songs was always loud, brassy and generally to a marching rhythm. Songs like *Wir fahren gegen England* and the *Horst Wessel Lied*, for example, speak for themselves. There was, however, one song that was so universally popular that it was adopted by British troops, especially by the Eighth Army, it was of course the haunting air of *Lilli Marlene*, but even that had a marching rhythm.

British songs, by contrast, were mostly comical or wistful. At the start of the war, the old songs from the previous conflict, such as *Tipperary*, were recycled, but soon fell out of use in favour of more modern tunes. Americans were astonished at the lack of patriotism as reflected in the British soldiers' songs. Ditties such as *'We're a Shower of Bastards'* were incomprehensible to the GIs. A quasi military unit, known as Entertainments National Services Association (ENSA), took performers to the troops. After a shaky start, Gracie Fields, the 'Lancashire Lass', and George Formby, 'the cheeky chappie,' with his banjo entertained the troops, but the greatest favourite was probably Vera Lynn who earned the unofficial title of the 'Forces Sweetheart' for her memorable repertoire. She sang songs guying the enemy with *'We'll hang out the washing on the Siegfried Line'*, *'Run rabbit, run rabbit, run run, run'* and *'Roll out the Barrel.'* However, her most popular songs were the sentimental ones such as *'There will be blue birds over the white cliffs of Dover'* and *'Smile as you wave me goodbye'*, and many others.

Naturally the troops had their own unprintable and generally obscene versions of popular songs. These usually dealt with the thieving propensities of their superior officers but there were also those which dealt in graphic detail with the anatomical peculiarities of the Nazi leadership or were concerned with impossible sexual fantasies common to large bodies of men deprived of feminine company for long periods. There was nearly always someone with a mouth organ, that supremely portable musical instrument, who was only too ready to get a sing-song going, whether on a route march or in the evening in a pub or the NAAFI.

In the autumn of 1944 when the Forres airfield at Balnageith was occupied by recently captured nationals who had been serving in the German army, Poles, Ukrainians and Russians, one of the Poles would play beautifully on a clarinet which was relayed over the camp's Tannoy (public address) system. One Sunday evening he performed *Ave Maria* and put into the haunting melody all the pathos and longing of a young man, far from home, who had supped on horrors which the good people of Forres could not even imagine. But, as the last beautiful notes faded away, a worthy pillar of the community was outraged that the purity of the Forres Sabbath had been violated by the public performance of a Popish tune. He protested vigorously to the Camp Commandant and never did the people of Forres hear that musician again.

Conscription

The problem of raising men for military service is probably as old as the history of warfare itself. But Napoleon, in 1798, first introduced the system of conscription, that is, compulsory enlistment in a military formation. The idea was adopted by Prussia in 1806. Britain introduced conscription in the First World War, so by the time the Second World War broke out the use of conscription was a foregone conclusion. Defined as 'legislation for all able bodied male citizens {and female citizens in some countries, such as Israel) to serve with the armed forces.' It became established in almost all European States. Modern conscription systems often permit alternative national service for conscientious objectors.

In Britain conscription was introduced for single men between the ages of 18 and 41 for the first time in March 1916 and for married men two months later but was discontinued after World War One. It was reintroduced in April 1939 when all men aged 20 became eligible for military training. The National Service Act passed in September 1939 made all men between ages 18 and 41 liable to service and in 1941 women were also liable to be called up for the women's services as an alternative to industrial service. Men reaching the age of 18 continued to be called up until 1960.

Owing to the absolute necessity of keeping most industries working to full capacity there were various occupational classes that were designated 'reserved occupations' whose members were exempt from call up. Agriculture is a typical example, where food production assumed a greater importance with the drastic reduction in imported foodstuffs. The formation of the Women's Land Army helped to address this situation. Later on during the war prisoners of war were also extensively employed in agriculture as farm labourers, a job at which the Italians were particularly adept though not so hard working as the German prisoners proved to be.

The shortfall in manpower created by the call-up of so many able bodied men was made good as far as possible by the return to work of many who had retired owing to age. Many men took on a second job voluntarily. The Air Raid Precautions (ARP) organization was largely manned by this means. Many men, having worked perhaps in a factory all day, spent the night hours on call as firefighters, fire-watchers or air raid wardens, others signed on as 'Specials' to augment the Police Force and so on.

Conscientious Objectors

People of military age whose conscience would not allow them to bear arms for the purpose of killing were subjected to a tribunal of inquiry; and if they were judged to be genuine cases they were directed to alternative war work. In March 1941 at the height of the air raids when hundreds of unexploded bombs were threatening to bring cities to a standstill 250 of these objectors volunteered to join the bomb disposal units. Safe disposal of unexploded bombs was possibly one of the most dangerous and stressful jobs undertaken during the war.

Other work available to the conscientious objectors was on the land or in forestry. When the war started, some 2% of those called up for military service registered as conscientious objectors. This fell during the course of the war so that by 1943 it was only 0.3% of the total. There were many who accepted directions to employment in the coal mines.

Gas Masks

Gas masks for all the population had been issued in the late summer of 1939 and with the declaration of war it had been made compulsory for everybody to carry them at all times. Little tots went off to school, their square cardboard boxes containing their respirator, dangling on a string. Some people covered their boxes with oil cloth and some, either insane or ostentatiously wealthy, covered theirs in mink.

Crime and Punishment

The war made everybody a criminal. Masses of regulations were introduced and wittingly or unwittingly, and mostly, unwittingly, everybody broke a regulation at some time.

It was illegal to swap your rations so that if you did not like sugar it was not allowed to swap your surplus sugar for your neighbour's bacon. If this ever happened nobody went to jail for it but, nevertheless it was technically illegal.

When Italy joined the war on the side of Germany in June 1940, this proved too much for plumber Martin Macdonald, a 58 year old veteran of the Boer War, who smashed up the Lido, but in view of his previous good conduct and having three sons in the army he was fined only £3. Not so leniently dealt with was Jessie McKinnon Henderson, Matron at Dr.Gray's Hospital in Elgin, who systematically stole rations from the patients for two years, from January 1942 until January 1944, to the extent that some 600lbs (over 250kg) of food was dispatched to an address in Paisley. She sent the parcels by rail and the station staff eventually wondered how a private individual could send so much stuff in wartime. The police were informed and opened a parcel and out fell a cornucopia of rationed foodstuff; ham, butter, margarine and eggs. She was sentenced to two month's imprisonment. Survivors of her regime describe how patients would count the grains of rice in their serving of rice pudding.

The black market and the spivs to operate it thrived. Americans bribed their way into the hearts and lives of the female population by producing nylon stockings. Americans could also supply .300 rimless ammunition as used by the Home Guard. British airmen, particularly rear gunners, could supply shotgun cartridges, much in demand in a rural community. Shooting with a shotgun allegedly improved skill with the four Brownings which was the gunners normal weapon. Again, this bartering or gifting was strictly illegal, but officialdom neither knew nor cared. After all, everybody was complicit in some way or another. Amongst legal activities was the shooting of peregrine falcons which occasionally preyed on carrier pigeons which, it was thought, may have been carrying military messages.

Amongst the minor misdemeanors of riding a bicycle without lights etc. there was a most brutal murder when on the evening of Thursday 26th August 1941 a girl of seventeen, Helen Margaret Shaw was battered by heavy stones about the head. Her body was found next morning on the bank beside the road to Pitgaveny by two children who were on their way to pick potatoes. The local constabulary were assisted by the Glasgow CID and meantime Dr.Gordon Thow had examined the body while Mr.Wilken took the official photographs. On Tuesday 31st August the police arrested James Wilson a soldier from Pinefield barracks, described in the censored press of the time as from a Highland Regiment.

Wilson stood trial at Inverness in November and there was little forensic evidence produced, the prosecution relying upon witness's statements. However, for every witness who said they had seen Wilson with the girl the defence produced a witness who declared that it was not Wilson with the girl but another soldier. The jury brought in the not unexpected verdict of not proven. But there is a not-proven sequel to this murder. On 1st January 1942 a James Wilson from a Highland Regiment, the Argyll and Sutherland

Highlanders, died in Cumbernauld. The name and age fit. Was this the accused?

Consequences and Casualties

As the Germans advanced across France the first army casualties were reported on 8th June 1940 when major D.S.Annand of The Gordon Highlanders was posted as killed while sergeant Joseph Mulholland of 40 Chanonry Road, Elgin was reported wounded. On the same day it was also reported that 273 evacuees were due in Elgin and compulsory billeting notices would be issued. In July of the same year the inhabitants of the Bruceland housing scheme built a communal air-raid shelter capable of holding 70 people and the same month the Government issued an appeal for housewives to hand in their aluminium pans in order to make Spitfires. Neighbours and towns vied with each other to see who could collect the most, but little was actually used and the stunt, for that is what it was, was primarily designed to get the public to act collectively and to feel that they were actually doing something positive towards the war effort. Another ploy was to take away the decorative railings around houses. This was not primarily for the iron content of the railings but as a gesture of communal support for the war effort. More useful in its iron content was the removal of the Crimean cannon from Lady Hill. Later, in 1944, a young lady by name of Allison Fordyce was killed by a tank at the east end of Elgin High Street.

Another idea, was to proclaim that the success of night fighter pilots, in particular, "Cats Eyes'" Cunningham, was due to their excellent night vision. This, of course, was said to be sustained by their diet of carrots. When small boys heard this news they ate their carrots with alacrity and this was most commendable for not only were carrots nutritious but they were home grown, and, if you did not like them raw or boiled you could always shred them down to bulk out cakes and puddings or use as filling for a sandwich. The emphasis on carrots and night vision was also intended to divert German attention away from the possibility that our night fighters were now using airborne radar.

Meanwhile, although there was no fighting and little bombing in Moray, there was still a steady attrition of manpower as accidents steadily claimed the lives of trainee airmen. Mostly the dead were discreetly shipped home to be buried in their native soil, but for those who came from abroad this was not possible, as the serried ranks of gravestones at Kinloss and Lossiemouth bear silent witness to their sacrifice. However, there is one aircrew from Moray who lie on the top of a remote West Highland mountain, their lonely graves rarely visited. Of course there were others on even more remote sites, such as Soay, one of the islands of the St.Kilda group.

On the 13th of April 1941, Anson N9857 with a crew of six took off from No.19 OTU Kinloss, on a routine training flight under the command of Flying Officer James Steyn, an experienced South African and a holder of the Distinguished Flying Cross. They flew north and then flew west towards Sutherland and into a severe snowstorm. Disorientated and with iced up wings the Anson ploughed into Ben More Assynt and, of the six crew, three died on impact while two died of exposure and Sgt. Jack Amery died while trying to get help.

Of the six crew, the captain was aged 23, his observer Pilot Officer William Drew was 28 while trainee observer Sgt. Charles Mitchell was the old man at 31. Sgt. Jack Amery was 20 while the instructor wireless operator was Flt. Sgt. Brendon Kenny, still only 20 but he had already been shot down over France where he evaded the Germans and returned to this country. Sitting beside him was trainee operator Flt.Sgt. Arthur Tompsett, also aged 20 and newly married to Anabeth Eva Amelia.

The airmen lay on the mountain for six weeks before the wreckage was found and the bodies were buried at the site and a cairn erected and eventually a cross and plaque were fixed while a supplementary memorial panel was installed at Inchnadamph old churchyard. In May 2003, thanks to the generosity of RAF Lossiemouth, the ageing relatives of two of the crew were air lifted to the site where their brothers died over sixty years previously. James Steyn, the pilot, lies far from his native Johannesburg, but except for the difference in temperature and wildlife the spot where he is buried is remarkably similar to the high veldt where he spent his youth.

Bombing

No enemy bombs were dropped on Elgin or Forres. A bomb was dropped near Drainie and damaged the school so that the pupils had to be sent on buses to Keam. Coastal towns, such as Portgordon, had a bomb or two dropped on them, but nothing sustained or serious. Aberdeen was not so fortunate and was bombed several times during the war. The worst raid was on the 21st of April 1943 when 98 people were killed and about 100 seriously injured and over 8,000 houses damaged.

Fraserburgh and Peterhead were also bombed several times and a total of 89 people killed, including 11 at Rosehearty. However, due to censorship and the consequent non-reporting of any incidents it is very difficult to record or comment on what actually occurred. One incident is well remembered and surprisingly well documented. On 22nd July 1940 a German bomber dropped several bombs on Duff House at Macduff and killed six German officers who were being held prisoner in the building. A further 70 were injured.

On 19th February 1941 a lone German aircraft dropped two bombs on Portknockie. There was a train puffing lots of black smoke at the railway station and the low flying aircraft released a bomb, which did not explode while the second missed its target and exploded near Seafield Street where three people were killed. On the 12th July 1941 a few bombs were dropped on Lossiemouth, severely damaging Dr.Brander's house and killing a family who had travelled from Plymouth to escape the Blitz. A lone bomb fell near Altyre, allegedly killing a rabbit. Another aircraft, presumably lost on the 4th August 1940, jettisoned its bombs in Glen Feshie while a similar incident occurred at Mulben.

By 1943 all industry was feeling the effects of four years of conscription for the forces. Women had been directed for two years into war work and there was some ill feeling that most of the Scottish women were sent to factories in the south and this encouraged many to opt for the Women's Land Army so that they could at least stay nearer home.

The coal mines were particularly short of labour and towards the end of 1943 conscripts were balloted and a small number, who were lucky or unlucky, were directed to the mines. These were known as Bevin Boys, named after Ernie Bevin the Minister for Labour. On Christmas Day 1943, (Christmas Day then was a normal working day), Robert McPherson of The Wards, Elgin received his call up for the mines.

Local Heroes

This is an idiosyncratic list and the only uniformity in it is that the names herein are in alphabetic order. Many were called but few were chosen. Some association with Moray, no matter how loose, is essential. There were many heroes and heroines in those days. Women, who put on a brave face as their men went to war or followed them onto the gun site, were all worthy of being especially remembered. The mothers who scrimped and saved and gave their children the rations allocated to the adult are all un-named and un-honoured heroines and, judging by the present generation's attitude, woefully neglected.

John Campbell Cowie is the first of our local heroes and is included because he is so typical of the many from Moray who fell without distinction and who were mourned at the time and are now ignored names on a war memorial. His service career was brief, his training inadequate, but for a few brief weeks his path and that of one of the authors crossed. One went on to death and the other to survival and, sixty years after John Cowie's death, it is fitting that his sacrifice should be commemorated as symbolic of all those others whose graves circle the globe.

John Cowie was born in 1923, the son of William and Jane Cowie of Lossiemouth. He enlisted in the RAF early in 1943, his service number being 1822254 and after his initial square bashing in Scotland he trained as an air gunner and had soon passed through his initial gunnery training and operational training and was posted to Snaith in Yorkshire where he was the rear gunner in a Halifax bomber of 51 Squadron. The Halifax was a four engined bomber with a service ceiling of 20,000ft. This was inferior to a Lancaster which could fly at 23,000ft but superior to the Stirling which could only manage 16,000ft. This discrepancy gave rise to the bitter comment by Stirling crews that they were in greater danger from bombs dropped by their higher flying comrades than they ever were from enemy flak.

On Friday 22nd October 1943, 51 Squadron took part in a 1,000 bomber raid on Kassel. Kassel is far into Germany beyond the Ruhr and to attack it meant flying over that heavily defended area. It is assumed that Cowie and his crew made it to the target and were on their way home when they fell prey to a German night fighter. Perhaps they were shot down by *Shräge Musik*, the recent introduction of upward firing machine guns into night fighters. The Halifax crashed in Holland and John Campbell Cowie lies buried at Antwerp. Beside his parents he left behind a baby daughter, Joan and his widow, Jeannie.

Alexander Mitchell Ferrier was an Elgin loon whose father had farmed at Longmorn and who, after attending the East End and West End schools joined the navy in 1936. He trained as a signalman and in May 1940 at Narvik in Norway he was serving on board a Polish destroyer the *Grom* when the ship was bombed and sunk and Leading Signalman Ferrier was awarded the Polish Cross of Valour for his bravery. Later he was at Dunkirk and Le Havre where he suffered severe shrapnel wounds to his back, carrying some of the shrapnel around with him for the rest of his days.

In 1942 he was walking along a street in Chatham, whilst waiting to be posted to a new ship, when he was approached by a naval commander who stopped Ferrier and asked him if he would like to join another officer on special duties. Ferrier was rightly flattered at receiving this special request and soon found himself with a select band of officers and ratings training to operate a two man chariot. This, in essence, was a torpedo, with a couple of seats on it so that the human crew could steer the torpedo and then set the charges. The idea was not new and had been reintroduced into modern warfare by the Italians, who were about to be paid the compliment of the idea being used against them.

On 3rd January 1943, with Lieutenant Richard Thomas Goodwin Greenland RNVR in the driving seat and Leading Signalman Alexander Mitchell Ferrier riding pillion, the intrepid pair slipped into Palermo harbour where the newly built Italian cruiser *Ulpio Traiano* was being prepared for service. Diving underneath the vessel the pair fixed limpet charges to the hull, set the fuses, and started to make their escape. The Cruiser was sunk and the navy pair were taken prisoner and initially incarcerated in an Italian Prisoner of War camp. They were transferred to the care of the Germans where Ferrier received some sort of electric treatment for his old back wounds.

For his bravery and devotion to duty, Ferrier was awarded The Conspicuous Gallantry Medal while Greenland was awarded the Distinguished Service Order. After the war, a new housing development in Bishopmill was named *Ferrier Terrace*, but few of the residents neither know nor care now why their street was so named.

Mora Scot, born Mora Joan Craig, graduated as a doctor from Aberdeen on the 15th July 1940 and went on to the Sick Childrens' Hospital to do her initial training. Then she moved to Elgin as an assistant to Dr. Gordon Scott whom she subsequently married in August 1942. Life was hectic then and had to be lived at an intensity which doctors today cannot imagine. The intensity reached its crescendo on the evening of Friday 9th February 1945 when Dr. Gordon Scott, the duty surgeon at Dr.Gray's hospital, was warned that casualties from the RAF at Dallachy were on their way. As the blood tub (RAF slang for ambulance) arrived, Dr. Mora Scott administered the anaesthetic while her husband, Gordon, carried out the life saving operations.

The pair worked throughout the night and saved the lives of Flying Officers Spink and Clifford and patched up others. Their heroic efforts were not broadcast then and are little known now, but there are children alive today whose grandfathers' owe their lives to the devotion to duty of Mora Scott and her husband Gordon.

Harbourne Mackay Stephen was born on 17th. April 1916 in the bank house at 151 High Street, Elgin where his father was the manager. Educated at Elgin, Edinburgh and Shrewsbury he joined Allied Newspapers in 1931. Later in the thirties he trained as a pilot with the Royal Air Force Volunteer Reserve (RAFVR) and was taking a conversion course on to Hurricanes at St.Athan when war broke out and he was posted to 605 Squadron as a Sergeant Pilot. He was commissioned in April 1940 and posted to 74 Squadron, then based at Hornchurch and commanded by that strict disciplinarian, "Sailor" Malan.

His squadron was in action at and around Dunkirk and Stephen shared in the destruction of several enemy aircraft. All during that summer, Stephen was in action and his activities were so conspicuous that he achieved the very first honour of a junior officer being awarded the Distinguished Service Order (DSO) in the field. He continued to fly against enemy aircraft until late in 1942 when increasing promotion and transfer to India removed him from the front line.

After the war he worked initially for Beaverbrook and eventually became Managing Director of the Daily and Sunday Telegraph. Made a CBE in 1985 he died in 2001 and a commemorative plaque has been erected on the Clydesdale Bank building in Elgin, the site of his birth.

Farquhar Stewart of 68 Newmill Road was a sergeant in the Seaforth Highlanders when on 27th May 1940, in action at Zillebeke, the three officers becoming casualties, Sewart took command of the company and ensured its safe withdrawal. For his gallantry in action he was decorated in the field with the Distinguished Conduct Medal (DCM)

George Preston Stronach was born on 4th December 1914 in Portgordon and went to the local school which he left when he was 14 to be apprenticed to the local butcher. However, his heart was set upon a career at sea and he signed up as a deck boy in 1932 and worked his way up through Able Seaman and then through the grades until he received his Master's Certificate in 1942 and joined the ship *Ocean Voyager* as Chief Officer.

The ship, with its cargo of petrol and ammunition, was at anchor in Tripoli on 19th March 1943 when she was attacked by enemy aircraft and set on fire. Fuel and ammunition were exploding and the captain was killed so Stronach took over as the officer in charge and gave the order to abandon ship. Several of the crew escaped but some 15 were trapped forward and Stronach, despite having been knocked unconscious by an earlier explosion, recovered sufficiently to rescue the men and see them into lifeboats.

He then searched the ship looking for further survivors and succeeded in rescuing the Second Officer, the Chief Engineer whose legs were broken and one of the Radio Officers, also with a broken leg. With No.3 hold and its cargo of 500 tons of 1000lb bombs on fire, Stronach thought it prudent to leave the ship himself, but just as he was about to do so he saw an unconscious greaser in the scuppers and he lowered this man with a line on to raft before finally abandoning his ship. He then dived into the water and swam to the raft and using a piece of wood as a paddle returned to the ship to ensure that all survivors were rescued.

He was awarded Lloyd's War Medal for Bravery at Sea and the George Cross. The George Cross was instituted on 28th September 1940 and is the highest decoration which can be given to a civilian and the ribbon is worn before all other decorations, with the exception of the Victoria Cross. Only 31 George Medals were awarded during the whole of the war. George Stronach subsequently worked on the Clyde as a pilot and retired to Acharacle and died at Inverness in December 1999.

Philip Underwood, was a Londoner, whose connection with Moray is that after narrowly failing to become a pilot he became a non-commissioned rear gunner and was sent to 20 OTU at Lossiemouth, there to crew up with his colleagues who would fly with him. On the 10th of December 1942, the crew shuffled into the briefing room, under the command of their skipper, Pilot Officer J.W.Heck, (an Australian, who came from one of the more desirable suburbs of Melbourne), to hear what their exercise would be. It was a clear frosty morning and their task was "a piece of cake". Fly east until over the North Sea then south, turn west to come back over land about Dundee then head north back home to Lossiemouth.

Once back over the mainland of Scotland the weather had deteriorated badly since take-off. It was now 10/10ths cloud and the aircraft started to ice up. The pilot tried to climb above the weather but the Wellington was not capable of this, so the 25 year old pilot made the fateful decision to come down and have a look. This manoeuvre, strictly prohibited but widely practised, led to many deaths and this was to be no exception. Too late the pilot skimmed over the shoulder of Ben Alder before crashing on the summit of Gael Charn, a 1049 metre high Munro which rises 6km to the south of Ardverikie on Loch Laggan. As the aircraft crunched into the mountainside so the massive deceleration killed all the crew members, except the rear gunner who was saved by the tail section breaking off completely before the deceleration could do its worst.

The daylight of a dark short day was rapidly fading as Underwood wrapped himself in his parachute to spend a cold and substantially sleepless night in the remains of his rear turret. Next morning he started to walk out but, unfortunately, took the wrong direction. If he had walked north he would have been at Ardverikie in 6km, but he headed south west and it was to be 14 squelching boggy kilometres, over some of the wildest country in Scotland, before he reached a shepherd's cottage. With assistance from Mr.Robertson, the shepherd, Phil Underwood made his way by train from Carrour to hospital at Fort William. After three weeks in hospital, he was sent home on leave and eventually returned to Lossiemouth.

But he was no longer the devil may care rear gunner but a frightened young man who had seen all his colleagues killed and was suffering from what is now widely recognised as post traumatic stress disorder. But the RAF did not see it this way. To officialdom he was a shirker and a scrounger and after 18 months of filling ammunition belts, in mid 1944 he was summoned to the dreaded Combined Reselection Centre on the Isle of Sheppey. There they charged him with lack of moral fibre and told him that if he did not go back to flying duties they would strip him of his stripes and gunner's brevet. Underwood fought the case and was supported by the medical staff so that he was one of the few who was saved the indignity of being labelled L.O.M.F. He kept his stripes and became a radio telephonist and, unknowingly, a local hero.

His five companions rest in scattered graves. One is buried at Soham, another at Preston, with a fellow Lancastrian at Liverpool. Only the pilot and 22 year old William Ernest Riley lie together at Lossiemouth.

They Also Served

Although not old enough for military service, the youth of Moray was mobilised and directed towards helping the war effort. Girls, in the Guides, rattled collecting tins gathering money for locally funded Spitfires and tanks also helped their mothers to knit comforts for the troops. There was an insatiable demand for sea-boot stockings for the navy and cap comforters and such for the army. They, along with the Rangers, also served in canteens, making sandwiches and serving teas etc. The Scouting service was under pressure as boys had a choice of three uniformed services they could join, though some scouts were enrolled as runners between air raid posts.

Every secondary school had an Air Training Corps where boys learnt aircraft recognition and the ability to pick out 'Beetle Juice' in the night sky. Betelgeuse is a bright star in the constellation of Orion and was then the main night time extra–terrestial guide to navigation. At Elgin Academy it was mainly the Lossiemouth loons who joined the Sea Cadets while the Army Cadet Corps mopped up the rest. The Corps fought many mock battles with the Home Guard and would spend occasional weekends at Fort George. As one ex-Corps reminisces "Cadet training was so tough it was a relief to join the army and be treated decently".

WORLD WAR II
IN MORAY

PART ELEVEN

MOVEMENT
CONTROL

Part Eleven
Movement Control

Security

During the war Security was everybody's business. In response to constant Government urging and reminders by way of posters everywhere, including the comic series by Fougasse amongst others, the nation became suspicious and tight lipped.

As one of the many precautions against the likelihood of enemy invasion all clues to location like signposts, were removed, milestones were buried and all name boards that showed place names were taken down and hidden away. This made map reading skill paramount for travellers outside their own areas, as many a junior subaltern found to his acute discomfort when trying to lead his unit in convoy across country.

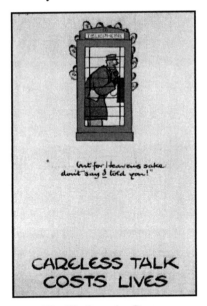

Fig 53. Security Poster
Courtesy IWM

In 1940 the Nation was gripped by an epidemic of 'spy hysteria'. All sorts of stories circulated about German parachutists disguised as nuns, Red Cross nurses, monks, policemen and so on. The situation was given some credence by a report in 'The Times' of 22 May 1940 about a press conference held by the Dutch Foreign Minister in London on 21 May when he is reported as having said that in Holland Germans had parachuted in so disguised. These troops were supposed to be the spearhead of invasion sent to create confusion behind the lines and to seize key installations. These rumours were given credence by the popular belief that the success of the 'blitzkreig' in France was largely due to the intervention of a fifth column of Pro-German collaborators. 'Spy hysteria' went hand in hand with 'fifth column mania' when there was widespread concern that the influx of refugees into Britain from the continent may have included a 'Trojan Horse' by way of enemy agents and saboteurs.

As a result of these various rumours the nation was in a state of heightened watchfulness and all during the summer of 1940 the main business of MI 5 was investigating reports of fifth column activity. The Government response to this period of public unrest was to pass a measure on 22 May known as the Treachery Bill. This new piece of legislation replaced the fourteenth century Treachery Acts. Rushed through parliament it provided a simplified procedure for dealing with those suspected of treachery, it closed a loophole in the law relating to non-resident aliens and made those convicted of contravention of its provisions liable to the death penalty.

During the so called 'phoney war' and during the blitzkreig into France, the German OPERATION YELLOW, the French were being regaled with subversive broadcasts from a radio station purporting to be run by Frenchmen from French territory and calling itself *La Voix de la Paix*. In Britain, as early as February 1939, the rumours of a fifth column were being fed steadily by subversive broadcasts to Britain from Nazi radio stations. A so called 'New British Broadcasting Station' started sending out programmes designed to confuse and create dissension. Using the signature tune 'The bonnie, bonnie banks of Loch Lomond' and signing off with the National Anthem it played on the theme of the coming invasion and the help the fifth column would provide to the German forces. There were three other enemy radio stations broadcasting subversive propaganda to Britain. Radio 'Caledonia', which used 'Auld Lang Syne' as a signature tune and concentrated on Scotland was first heard on 18 July. 'Workers Challenge' targeted shopfloor workers from 8 July and the 'Christian Peace Movement' beamed its programme from Hamburg at church-going people. These broadcasts continued throughout the war.

It is interesting to note that the British broadcasts to the enemy concentrated on Black propaganda to provide misleading intelligence with the purpose of strategic deception of the military planners rather than subversive propaganda aimed at the civilian population. It was about this time that the idea, enthusiastically endorsed by Churchill, of forming 'stay behind' parties of trained saboteurs, whose job it would be in event of invasion to go underground. They would lie low until they could emerge stealthily in rear of the enemy and wreak havoc behind his lines. The British Resistance was formed as a covert branch of the Home Guard, called Auxiliary Units, under the command of General Gubbins.. Plans were also prepared to move five sensitive and essential Ministries of Government to prepared secure accommodation as soon as invasion became certain. The plans, under the code name of Operation BLACK MOVE, were later aborted.

Arrangements had been made that the signal for invasion by airborne forces would be the ringing of church bells, From 13 June 1940 the bells would only be rung on the instructions of the police or the military. As everyone knows the Invasion, codenamed SEALION, never happened. Hitler finally called it off on 15 September 1940. But there were two false alarms. and church bells were rung The first occurred on the night of 13-14 August 1940 when about eighty unmanned enemy parachutes were dropped, with sabotage and other subversive material, in the midlands of England.. No personnel were discovered and it was assumed to have been an enemy propaganda exercise.

The second occasion was on the evening of 7th September 1940 when signs indicated that invasion was imminent and the appropriate codeword CROMWELL was flashed to units This was a stand-by signal but was misunderstood by some units to mean that the invasion had started. It was soon realised that it was a false alarm although many Auxiliary units went to ground and some bridges were blown up in place. Dr John MacDonald recalls that at the time he was at home from Aberdeen University and was serving in the Elgin platoon of the Home Guard. Six of them were enjoying a game of cards in a small lean-to overlooking the Kintrae Brae when a despatch rider roared up the narrow track shouting 'The Germans have landed.'

Travelling

Travelling during the war was officially discouraged. Posters demanded 'Is Your Journey Really Necessary?' From the start petrol was rationed, limiting monthly travel to 320 km. The inevitable result was a black market with fuel selling at up to four times its legal price. Petrol was dyed red in an effort to limit the illegal use Some users tried other dodges such as adding paraffin to the petrol with varying results, always poor. Some cars tried running on mains gas from a large inflatable bag carried on the roof of the vehicle. Others even tried running on gas produced from a small furnace on the back of the machine, burning wood chips. After March 1942 petrol was no longer available for private use and most people gave up and laid their cars up on blocks 'for the duration' In spite of these restrictions the Government decreed that it was an offence to leave a motor vehicle unattended without immobilising it, the recommended method was to remove the rotor arm from the distributor.

Shank's pony became popular for many journeys and the sale and repair of bicycles become a popular pastime. Buses were overloaded and it was always difficult for the conductress, aka clippie, to fight her way past the standing passengers to issue tickets.

From then on people were to rely on public transport with all its inconveniences and discomfort produced by overcrowding and irregular timekeeping for which the excuse was invariably 'there is a war on!' Travel by train was particularly difficult. The regional railway companies were all taken over by the government to cope with the enormous logistic problems of moving personnel and material round the country with the maintenance of the war effort as its priority.

Internment

Civilian nationals of those countries with which we were at war, namely Germany and Italy, were interned by order of the Home Office under the provisions of the peacetime Aliens Order amended by various Orders in Council. The Geneva Conventions did not cover non-combatant enemy aliens. However, when the war began the Committee of the International Red Cross obtained from the belligerent countries an agreement that interned civilians, including merchant seamen, should have the same status as prisoners of war (Dear 1995: 569).

Aliens for internment were arrested by the Police and passed to the military for custody. In 1939 there were about 70,000 enemy aliens in Britain of whom about 55,000 were refugees from the Nazi regime in Germany and Austria. A large proportion of these were Jews and the majority of them were in London and the south of England, which gives an indication of the problem that confronted Sir John Anderson, the Home Secretary at the time.

In Morayshire there were very few, nationals or persons of German or Austrian origin. However, there were many persons of Italian origin throughout Morayshire. By the end of September 1939 some 120 tribunals had been set up in various parts of the country charged with the task of sorting the genuine refugees from those who might not be friendly to Britain. These were classed as non-refugees. The tribunals sorted the aliens into three categories: 569, Category 'A' considered a danger to the country and to be interned, 6,782 'B' exempt from internment but subject to restrictions, and 66,000, 'C' friendly and exempt from both internment and restrictions.

As the war progressed and the possibility of invasion came closer the official attitude towards aliens hardened fuelled by public demand and the fears, not far removed from panic, about the menace of a Fifth Column.. The provisions of Regulation 18b of the Defence (General) Regulations 1939 were tightened up and the Registration regulation of 1920 meant that every alien was already known to the Police. A Certificate of Registration, to be produced on demand, was issued to each one with their particulars and a photograph. Further internment of suspected aliens followed. On 10 June 1940 the Police made arrests of all males listed between the ages of 17 and 70. After being taken to the Police Station these detainees were then handed over to the Military for transfer to detainment camps. Transit camps were set up in Edinburgh at Woodlea and Milton Bridge, also at Huyton in Liverpool where detainees were taken en route to permanent camps established at Douglas in the Isle of Man.

The organisers of the British union of Fascists were taken into custody along with Sir Oswald Mosley and other prominent members of the 'Blackshirt' organisation. In July 1940, 1,373 persons were interned, but most were released by early 1941. Many internees were confined in camps set up on race courses, or in partially completed housing estates. On the Isle of Man the empty boarding houses and hotels were glad to accept them for a payment of 3 shillings (fifteen pence) per head per day. At Douglas the camps were established using the hotels Granville, Palace and Metropole. At Ramsey 57 boarding houses w commandeered for internees.

Some internees were sent abroad and 721 people mainly 156 Germans 486 Italians and 79 British, lost their lives when one ship, the *SS Arandora Star* on passage to Canada sank in about 30 minutes after being torpedoed at about 1.30 am on 2 July 1940 by Gunther Prien in U47. The same commander who, on 14 October 1939 had sunk the *HMS Royal Oak* whilst she lay at anchor in Scapa Flow.(Pieri: 1997; 29).The survivors were settled in camps in Canada. Other shipments went to Australia in the *SS Dunera* where their treatment caused an outcry in Parliament.

Fig 54. The ill-fated SS Arandora Star
Courtesy Mrs Chiappa

After the tragedy of the *SS Arandora Star* public opinion changed again and turned against the Government policy and the callous way in which it had been implemented. The well authenticated stories of unnecessary hardship and even of tragedies occurring as a result of the mass-internment so precipitately and inhumanely executed were well ventilated in the popular press. The reason for the whole sorry episode is not far to seek. In May 1940 the Government had to take every reasonable precaution against the perceived menace of the Fifth Column.

The failure was not in adopting a harsh and vigorous policy, but in the insensitive and inhuman way in which it was carried out. The lack of forward planning inevitably meant that the hurried execution of the policy was bound to be rough and ready leading to many muddles with unnecessary suffering and hardship. 'It is a sad story of panic and often bungling on the part of the authorities which, although it can be easily explained as a consequence of war, it cannot easily be excused'

Overnight the Italians in Scotland were looked on as enemies and they could scarcely believe it until they saw their properties being vandalised and the police came to their doors to arrest them. It was a traumatic shock to find themselves suddenly interned as possible dangerous fifth columnists.

In spite of the campaign against careless talk, in late January 1940 a press campaign encouraged a mood of xenophobia and a 'spy mania' swept the country resulting in a Home Office order barring all aliens, between 16 and 70, from 'protected areas' round the coasts in England and the North of Scotland, Orkney, Shetland and the Firth of Forth. In May 1940 with the situation deteriorating in Norway, Belgium and Holland the Home Office directed the immediate temporary internment of all male Germans and Austrians in England and Scotland. This was extended on 12 May to include movement restrictions on all other male aliens in the same age group regardless of nationality.

Fig 55. A Security Poster
HMSO

Most camps were ringed with barbed wire and had watch towers. They were usually guarded by thee Pioneer Corps troops commanded by Officers from the Intelligence Corps. In June 1940 Mussolini finally decided to come down off the fence on the side of the Axis and embraced Hitler as a partner in the war, which was apparently going in Germany's favour. Thus, at a stroke, Italians were changed into enemy nationals eligible for internment. There were few towns or villages throughout Scotland that did not have a well-established Fish and Chip shop or Café. In Moray there were many such families of Italian extraction mostly engaged in the Café and Ice Cream Parlour trade. There were a few others in various different trades and occupations.

In Elgin there were the families Bonici, Civiera, Conti, Giandria. Guidi, Janarelli, Lunardi, and Zanre (JGR Mitchell, *pers commn*). In Lossiemouth and in Huntly there was the family Rizza. In Forres there was the families Miele and the family Zanre which returned to Italy as soon as Mussolini declared war. In Buckie and district there was the family Jannetta. In Grantown on Spey, which was part of Morayshire during the war, there were two Italian families, Arccari with a café in the Square and Demacio with a café in the High Street.

From August 1940 internees began to be released and by February 1941 more than 10,000 were freed and by the summer only about 5,000 were left in the camps. Many of those released joined the British armed forces, mainly the Pioneer Corps or the auxiliary services such as the Auxiliary Fire Brigade or the ARP.

Gordonstoun

The ideals that formed the core of the philosophy of Gordonstoun School originated in the ideas of Plato and his *Republic*. Plato's philosophy was absorbed in Germany by Dr. Kurt Hahn, a friend and confidant of Prince Max of Baden who placed his castle at Salem in south Germany, near Lake Constance, at the disposal of Hahn for the foundation of a school for the children of the intellectual and artistic. The first pupil was Max Baden's son. The school survived and developed but was an early victim of Nazi oppression. Even before Hitler became Reich Chancellor in 1932, Kurt Hahn became a marked man when he wrote publicly condemning the brutal murder of a Communist by five S.A men. Dr Hahn was arrested in March 1933 and was only released on the personal intervention of the Moray born Prime minister, Ramsay Macdonald. Later that year Hahn fled to London and was persuaded to start a Salem-like school in Britain. This he did, selecting dilapidated Gordonstoun as the unlikely site for his courageous adventure.

The school gradually increased in numbers and financial stability until 1939 when ten of the teaching staff left to join the forces. However there were German pupils at the school and Germans on the staff, and xenophobia has long been a well-developed characteristic of the British public. The invasion of Norway closely followed by the attack on the Low Countries brought matters to a head. Five masters were interned including the gentle and obviously harmless Dr. Richter, and there was strong pressure from the Regional Commissioner for Scotland, (Tom Johnston M.P. until succeeded by Lord Rosebery in Feb. 1941), to intern Kurt Hahn as well. But Hahn was a naturalised British citizen and despite Churchill's exhortation to 'collar the lot' he was allowed to continue, but not at Gordonstoun.

Regulations had already been introduced to prohibit camping or any temporary accommodation within five miles of the coast and, to the official mind it was intolerable that Gordonstoun school, with its suspected founder, should continue in such a sensitive area. Besides, the army wanted Gordonstoun House for its own purposes. Thanks to the generosity of Lord Davies who placed his mansion at 'Plas Dinam' in central Wales at the disposal of Hahn, the school was successfully transferred there in 1940. In 1942 a pupil of the school founded the Gordonstoun Fire Service and this, considerably extended, survives to this day. Later in the war, the Germans detained in the Isle of Man and in Canada were released and all were able to devote their considerable talents to helping the British war effort. Several former pupils paid the supreme sacrifice and their names are suitably recorded, irrespective upon which side they fell.

Enemy Agents captured in Moray

In the context of both first and second World Wars, agents inserted into Britain by Germany for the purposes of espionage and sabotage appear, at least from the British record, to have been singularly unsuccessful. The training and briefing of their agents appears to have been woefully inadequate and exhibits a degree of ignorance and naiveté on the part of their masters. 'It is surprising that the German Abwehr adopted a technique of espionage which was so crude and inept that it was unlikely to yield any results, which could justify the expenditure involved'.

The explanation may be that the Abwehr controllers at the Agent level were simply the victims of their own propaganda. They told their spies that they would have no problem moving about as the country was in a turmoil with refugees everywhere fleeing from the bombing of their cities. John Moe recounts in his book (Moe 1986:101) his surprise at being sent to spy on Britain without any maps. Of his fellow trainee spies he says, 'they did not stand a chance; well, not if they had received the same advice and preparation that we had....we were convinced that we would never survive more than a day or two as genuine spies'.

According to *The Double Cross System,* (by Sir John Masterman, one-time Vice Chancellor of Oxford University and the Chairman of the Twenty Committee), the German master spy Arthur Owens, a Welshman, was in reality a double agent working for MI5 in World War Two. Because the Germans notified Owens in advance when they were sending in an agent they were invariably successfully captured on arrival. Most of them when offered the alternative of 'work for us or face a firing squad' were not surprisingly turned into double agents enabling the German espionage service to be effectively run and controlled from Britain by the British. Owens had been ostensibly operating for his German controller, Maj. Ritter of the Abwehr, since 1936, under the code name 'Johnny'. His MI6 code name was 'Snow', a partial anagram of his name.

Not one of the German Agents operating in Britain was sending entirely straightforward messages to the Abwehr or the RSHA. Every one of them had been 'turned' and was operating under British controllers sending only the information that we wanted the enemy to know. Some of the information was true, some of it was faked. The true information was usually known to the enemy from other sources already published but mixed in with it were the misleading dummy messages intended to confuse and misinform. The unimportant real news lent colour and apparent reliability to the false news and the Germans, who, as Churchill said, 'firmly believed the evidence we obligingly put at their disposal' (Kahn. 1987; 368)'

German sources allege that, in July 1944, 260 men and women agents were dropped and between June 1944 and March 1945, 600 Abwehr agents were dropped behind enemy lines. (*Unternehmen Moewe*. stahlbrandt.com) Spies caught by the Police or the Military were charged under the terms of the Treachery Act of 1940, which carried a mandatory death penalty for persons convicted of spying. British records show that during World War Two, 46 countries provided spies for Germany and 30 agents came to Britain clandestinely by parachute, submarine, seaplane or small craft. Sixteen spies were executed, 15 by hanging, 9 at Wandsworth Prison, 6 at Pentonville Prison and one by firing squad at the Tower of London. Some were turned to act as double-agents, many other enemy agents were interned or imprisoned for the duration of the war. After the executions, 'to deter others', the policy for dealing with spies was changed to the establishment of a human reference database for use in interrogating and/or indoctrinating others.

Two Norwegian nationals, code names 'Mutt' and 'Jeff', or known to the Germans as 'Ja' and 'Tege', were landed from a Blohm and Voss seaplane in the Moray Firth near Crovie in Banffshire on 7th April 1941. As later reported in the Aberdeen Press and Journal, they were named Helge Moe and Tor Glad and had come from Norway where they had worked in the German Postal Censorship Department in Oslo. As patriotic Norwegians, (Glad had been a sergeant in the army), they sought ways of continuing the fight against Germany and conceived the idea of trying to become spies with a view of being sent to Britain where they could give themselves up and offer their services as double agents. Accepted by the Germans and trained by the Abwehr they were sent to Scotland under the operational code name 'Hummer Nord III' briefed to carry out acts of sabotage by starting fires in food dumps and factories and sever power lines to create panic and disruption. Both men promptly gave themselves up and offered to work for Britain.

They were sent to London and interrogated by MI 5. Helge Moe had been born in London and became a most useful double agent working for Britain, but Tor Glad, aka 'Jeff' proved to be unreliable and was later interned in the Isle of Man at Camp WX and later in Dartmoor where he remained until the end of the war. His role was taken over by a British agent trained to copy Glad's morse 'signature'. Their role ceased in 1943 when it was thought that they had been compromised and in any case their usefulness declined after the invasion of Normandy.

To sustain a double agent's credibility it was occasionally necessary to carry out, or seem to carry out, the orders of their masters. Mutt and Jeff carried out three acts of sabotage carefully arranged by the double-cross (XX .or 'Twenty' as it was known) committee. The first, under the code name GUY FAWKES in November 1941, was to blow up a warehouse depot at Wealdstone near Hendon. This was a store full of spoiled sugar supplies that could be readily sacrificed The second in the same year, code name BROCK, was to blow up some Nissen huts, which were part of a disused Army camp. The third, BUNBURY, was the 'sabotage' of an abandoned electricity generating station at Bury St. Edmonds in August 1943.

They were so successful that the Germans agreed to several parachute re-- supply drops codenamed, PORRIDGE and HAGGIS. One of 'Mutt's' final operations was to ask for a further parachute drop of equipment and money. The Germans agreed and it was codenamed operation OATMEAL It was arranged that they would use Loch Strathbeg (NGR NK 070590) just south of Fraserburgh as the drop zone. So, on the night of 20 February 1943 the drop was successfully carried out. The RAF had been warned not to interfere. A quantity of captured SOE material and a sum of £400 was dropped. On the first of the following month, by coincidence, work began to build a new airfield precisely where the drop had been made. Unfortunately the Germans had decided to load their aircraft with bombs, as well as the agents' equipment, and it went on to bomb Fraserburgh demolishing houses and killing an eleven year old boy named Laurence McKay Kerr.

Each sabotage act was actually carried out by our own explosives experts from Special Branch and in conditions of great secrecy so that the authorities would be fooled as well as the enemy. Care was taken to ensure that the sabotage was factually reported in the Press and the news reached the Abwehr in a normal fashion. These were all clever fictions wholly devised by MI5 and supported by fake evidence on the ground to fool the inevitable reconnaissance planes sent to check on the spies' reports. Major Jasper Maskelyne of the Royal Engineers' Camouflage Experimental Station, who was responsible for previous large-scale military optical illusions, ingeniously created the misleading dummy evidence on the ground.

Jasper Maskelyne, born 1902, was a Music Hall illusionist whose talents were recruited by the Royal Engineers Camouflage Unit and was sent to Egypt where he created illusions to deceive the enemy. To prevent the bombing of Alexandra Harbour a dummy harbour was created at night by setting up in the desert a pattern of lights duplicating the harbour installations which were then blacked out The deception was entirely successful in misleading the enemy pilots who bombed the sand dunes. Other illusions were equally successful, like persuading Rommel, before the battle of Alamein, that the attack would be launched from the south rather than from the north. Maskelyne's repertoire included the use of lights and mirrors to create his illusions so successfully. (http://www.cometamagico.com.ar/maskelyne2.htm). The double-cross system was operated by MI5 throughout World War Two and succeeded in the total compromise of all German spies who operated in Britain. The 'turned' agents who chose the option of working for Britain rather than face the death penalty were allowed to continue their role as German spies but all the information they transmitted to their Nazi spy-masters was carefully composed and controlled by MI5.

Although taking place far from Moray it is nevertheless interesting to note that the crowning piece of large-scale deception achieved was the operation codenamed 'BODYGUARD'. This was designed to make the enemy believe that the invasion of Europe would be launched across the narrowest part of the English Channel from south eastern England directly at the Pas de Calais. A phantom army was created in East Anglia comprised of dummy tanks, planes and troops backed up by a constant stream of dummy radio traffic. That such an organisation would have created and then reported by the double-cross spies convinced the Abwehr and Hitler that the Normandy landing was only a diversion. This misinformation tied up valuable enemy forces and kept them away from the Normandy bridgehead during the critical first days of the landing contributing greatly to its success. (Wesr.1981:210ff).

Two men and a woman arrived, from Stavanger, in a Blom and Voss flying boat (also described as a twin-engined He 115 seaplane. Kahn:1978:353). They came ashore in a rubber dinghy (see Appendix 7) at Portgordon, Moray, in the early hours of 30th September 1940. Their bicycles, which had been stolen from the basement of the deserted British embassy in Bergen and on which they were supposed to travel the six hundred miles to reach London, were lost overboard in rough water when transferring to the dinghy from the flying boat. The woman later, under interrogation, was unnerved and like most women in espionage broke by instalments and admitted that this was in fact their second journey to Scotland. The first attempt by fishing boat from Aalesund had to be aborted because of bad weather. The first time the party had included a Norwegian journalist named Edvardsen who was left behind but came on later and confirmed this story after he too was captured.

Their orders were to get to London but the loss of their bicycles was a set back and so, on arrival, they split up and one man and the woman, carrying their luggage, found their way to the railway station at Portgordon where they arrived at about 7.30 a.m.. The woman was named Vera Eriksen and was described on her identity card as a Vera Cottani-Chalbur a Danish refugee claiming to be a widow born in Siberia and living in London. The man was Karl Theo Drücke who had assumed the name Francois de Deeker as a French refugee from Belgium also living in London.. At the station their behaviour and appearance aroused the suspicions of John Donald the stationmaster when Vera asked 'what is the name of this station, please?' The station name, like all place names in the country, had been obliterated. Donald noticed that their legs and feet were still wet from wading ashore from their rubber dinghy and they had to consult a wall timetable before buying two tickets. The porter, John Geddes, was sent to fetch the local police constable PC Robert Grieve.

After examining the identity cards made out in continental writing and after a brief interrogation they were taken to the Police Station where Grieve telephoned his superior, Inspector John Simpson at nearby Buckie. After further interrogation, when the woman, who had previously given the name of the Duchesse de Chateau-Thierry of Dorset House London, as a reference, asked to speak privately to the Inspector, and referred him to a Capt. King who worked at the War Office and who would vouch for her. Capt. King turned out to be Max Knight for whom Vera had worked as an informant in London. Now the matter was taken up by the Regional Security Liaison Officer (RSLO), Major Peter Perfect, who was summoned from Edinburgh. Vera now turned themselves in and they were arrested., she disclosed that she was supposed to escort the two agents, Drücke and Wälti to London. It was clear that they were enemy agents and a search of their luggage turned up conclusive evidence that they had come equipped with items for espionage. These included a pistol and ammunition, a wireless and accessories including batteries, a coding device, graph paper, English money and a list of place names, that turned out to be airfields, and a piece of German sausage.

The capture was reported to police HQ at Banff and a search of the shore line, where an inflated four-man rubber dinghy was found drifting towards Cluny

Harbour Buckie, followed by enquiries revealed that another man had walked into the railway station at Buckpool at about 6.50 a.m where enquiring for a train for Aberdeen he was directed to Buckie railway station one mile further down the road. At Buckie he had bought a ticket for Edinburgh and caught the next train to Aberdeen. Major Perfect now telephoned the Chief Constable in Edinburgh with a request that the Aberdeen train was to be met and the passenger intercepted, but the call was too late and a major search operation was started in Edinburgh. Arriving in Edinburgh he had a wait for the next London connection and went to a hairdresser and had a shave and spent some time in a cinema. Returning to the station to collect his left luggage he was ambushed by Detective Superintendent Merrilees (later to become Chief Constable of Edinburgh and Peebles) and several policemen disguised as porters. When searched he was found to be armed with a loaded 6.35mm Mauser pistol and a flick-knife. Drücke also had a flick-knife, a weapon not commonly found in Britain at that time.

Fig 56. Portgordon Station Looking NW over the
beach where the spies may have come ashore.

(Buckpool Station was similar in design)

Photo: Buckie Dist. Fishing Heritage Museum

After capture all three were taken under escort to New Scotland Yard and handed over to Inspector F. Bridge of Special Branch. The men were sent to Camp 020 and Vera Eriksen was housed in Holloway's 'E' wing. They were interrogated by Lt. Col. Hinchley-Cooke from MI 5 and statements were taken. In June 1941 after a trial 'in camera' at the Old Bailey before Mr Justice Asquith, brother of the former Prime minister, with Sir (later Lord) William Jowitt prosecuting, the two men were sentenced to death and hanged at HM Prison Wandsworth on 6th August 1941.

No proceedings were brought against the woman Vera Eriksen and after she was imprisoned in Holloway for the rest of the war she faded out of the story. 'Maybe she was able to be of some use to our authorities' it was speculated. In some reports the woman was said to have changed her name and settled in the Isle of Wight after the war. It is also suggested that Eriksen had been a pre-war part-time informant for MI5 and she escaped punishment. What is certain is that there does not appear to be any record of Vera's execution. It eventually transpired that her real name was Schalburg.

A letter marked 'VERY SECRET AND PERSONAL' was sent to Churchill on 31 October 1940 by Lord Swinton, head of the Swinton Committee set up by Churchill and responsible for Security and Special operations. The letter reports the arrival, on 25 October 1940, of three men who landed from a rubber boat near Nairn in what is described as 'Colvin Bay', clearly a misnomer.

PC James Collie, the police officer stationed at Auldearn who had been instructed to search the Nairn beach for a boat, reported to his Chief Constable of Moray and Nairn with a full description of the rubber dinghy he found on the Culbin Sands about 400 yards North West of the Old Bar fishing bothy. The boat was identified, by a RAF Intelligence Officer as a type known to have been used by the Luftwaffe. The part above the waterline, originally yellow, had been painted green. There was also an aluminium paddle with German lettering on it.

The men, who claimed to be refugees, told the police that they had been brought by boat, the Boreas, from Aalesund.(another report says Stavanger) They were arrested and taken to Nairn. It was later learned under interrogation that they had arrived by plane from Stavanger. They were identified as Sigmund Lund, (also identified as Legwald Lund. MI5 *pers. comm.*) a Norwegian ship's Captain aged 50 who had assaulted a German policeman and Gunnar Edvardsen a Norwegian journalist aged 33, who had both been press-ganged.. Also, Otto Joost a German from the Saar, aged 39, who had fought for the Spanish government in the Civil War.

Lund had a Norwegian passport but the others had no papers. Between them they had various sums in English money totalling £250. They appeared to have no luggage, instruments or maps. They stated that they had two bicycles but they had to jettison them in order to lighten their boat which had very little freeboard. They were tasked to pose as refugees and to travel about the country sabotaging communications by cutting telephone wires. Under interrogation Joost confessed that he had buried his insulated wire cutters in a sand dune at the beach. They said that the invasion was expected, possibly on November the tenth. MI5 concluded that like many other espionage enterprises that were launched against this country from Norway there was considerable doubt about the missions they were expected to perform. It seems likely that they were intended to act as short-term agents and to create as much confusion and spread alarm wherever the opportunity occurred. None of these agents had very specific instructions and the fact they retained no means of communication, were inadequately briefed and equipped suggested that they were clearly regarded by the Abwehr as short-term agents.

Edvardsen had originally been intended to travel with the Eriksen party which arrived at Portgordon on 30 September 1940 (*vide suprs*). It was concluded that they were very low grade agents not likely to be entrusted with accurate inside information and that they may have been encouraged, as other captured agents were, with an assurance that the invaders would shortly be joining them. On return to Norway on 15 November 1946 after spending the war in a British prison Edvardson was arrested and tried in Oslo on 10 June 1947 where he was sentenced to imprisonment with hard labour for two years and to loss of civil rights for ten years.

MI5 also record a Norwegian agent, Nicolay Steen Marinius Hansen, who arrived by parachute in Morayshire on the night of 30 September / I October 1943. At 0500 hrs. he surrendered to the drivers of two fish lorries loaded with Aberdeen herrings who fetched the police, and Hansen handed over two radio transmitters, one English and one German.. He said that he had been instructed to hand over the English transmitter as evidence of his desire to co-operate but to conceal the German one until he had been set at liberty by the British. He was then to report on all matters of military interest.

Hansen was imprisoned in Camp 020 where he was interrogated and it was revealed that he had secret writing materials hidden in a small rubber bag secreted in a hollow tooth. When the tooth was extracted the materials were discovered. Apparently he had already chewed and swallowed the faulty stopping and contents of another hollow tooth when he was given his first meal at the camp. If the materials had been discovered Hansen was instructed to explain them as a suicide portion. Clearly a slow-witted agent of very low quality and of limited intellect Hansen was unsuitable for employment as a double-agent and was retained in captivity at Camp 020 until the end of hostilities.

On 4th October another German Agent parachuted into Scotland. He was allotted the codename GANDER by MI5. He was provided with a wireless transmitter but did not have a wireless receiver. He had a ration book and a forged identity card by which MI5 identified him from information already taken from other agents. Although dressed in civilian clothes he was carrying a Luftwaffe uniform and paybook. His brief was to transmit weather information from the midlands of England and to report on morale. He was told by the Abwehr to expect the German invasion forces in about two weeks when he was to rejoin them. Presumably that was why he was carrying his uniform. He agreed to become a double agent but lacking a wireless receiver he was of little value. He escaped prosecution and was imprisoned until the end of the war.

There are unsubstantiated reports of further cases. One was of two men who came down the River Findhorn, presumably having parachuted in, possibly over Dava Moor, with a mission to gather intelligence about airfields near Forres and perhaps to carry out sabotage. They incautiously lit a fire in a deserted quarry and the smoke gave them away to a Home Guard patrol which took them prisoner and handed them over to the Police at Forres.

There are reports of two more suspected agents (men ?) who tried to buy food in a Lossiemouth Baker's shop and being unfamiliar with the value of the British money they aroused suspicion, and were arrested by the Police. Also in Lossiemouth it is reported that a young man wearing British battledress with CANADA flashes on the sleeves was found by two schoolboys on the shore asking questions about minefields and airfield. He too was arrested by the Police and taken to an identity parade at a nearby Canadian Forestry Unit. There is no further information as to whether he was an agent or simply a deserter. Unfortunately, despite every effort, these reports remain unconfirmed.

Sadly it has proved impossible to obtain any comprehensive official information on this whole subject from any of the acknowledged sources. It is a subject which being covert, was shrouded in secrecy at the time and is still largely inaccessible. The majority of the foregoing information comes from 'After the Battle No 11', local press reports and from sources quoted. The Public Record Office at Kew, London and MI5 have both been of assistance. Several witnesses were able to provide their personal recollections of events but they were young children at the time and their interest was cursory and their memories suffered from the intervening decades.

From interrogations and especially from their complete control of enemy agent communications, the British gradually grew aware that they had captured every single German spy on the island. Tight immigration controls and Allied air superiority, which blocked any comprehensive German aerial reconnaissance, assisted by Enigma and Allied cryptographic expertise, which denied the Germans any chance of breaking top Allied messages, prevented the enemy from discovering what was really going on and contributed hugely to the success of the many schemes of deception.

The question often asked is why did the German's espionage system in Britain fail so completely? Possibly in the failure to provide long-term peacetime preparation. In practice the odds against the spy in wartime are great especially whilst the country is gripped with an anti-spy hysteria. This makes everybody into a potential counter-intelligence agent. The restrictions on free movement hinder the spy and make him conspicuous. As it became more and more obvious that the Germans were losing the war their spies began giving themselves up. The quality and aptitude of the spies arrested in Moray was so abysmally poor that the suspicion arose that they were perhaps being sacrificed to allay any possible suspicion about more successful and highly trained operatives, but the record proves this to be unfounded.

Recent research reveals that British successes in spy-catching may have had more to do with Major General Erwin Von Lahousen than had been realised. Erwin Von Lahousen was part French, his full name was Von Lahousen-Vivremont. He was second in command to Admiral Canaris with whom he was actively participating in the plot to assassinate Hitler. Von Lahousen took pains to select for spying missions those Nazi fanatics he was not sorry to lose. His agents were not the highest level of spies and their unsophisticated procedures, cursory training and ignorance of the British way of life led inevitably to their early capture. MI5 took full credit for the successful capture of enemy agents when, in fact, they were casually dumped into the yawning mouth of the Britsh lion. Erwin Von Lahousen survived the war and testified against the Nazis at Nuremburg in 1946 but died in 1955. (http://www.angelfire.com/dc/1spy/Lhousen.html)

Forres - the Fascist and the Field Marshall

In 1873 in the village of Fulford in Yorkshire was born Cicely Mary Godman, daughter of Major General Richard Temple Godman and his wife, Eliza Mary de Crespigny. In June 1899 she married Alexander Edward, distiller in Moray and laird of Sanquhar. Sanquhar lies about two kilometres to the south of the town and was much enlarged in 1863. Lying on high ground it has magnificent views over Forres and across the Culbin sands.

Alexander was a good Laird and gave generously to local charitable causes, endowing a number of council houses in the years following the First War. His wife, the expected staunch Unionist and Conservative, drifted further to the right and became involved with the British Union of Fascists. In May 1940, Churchill fearful of the work of a Fifth Column authorised the seizure and detention of 436 persons, of whom 150 were described as 'prominent' under Defence Regulation 18b. Two of the first three persons on this list were cousins by marriage of Clementine Churchill, the prime minister's wife. (Brown.1988.270). They included Sir Oswald Mosley (who was married to Diana, one of the notorious Mitford sisters). He was an aristocratic mobster who joined The British Union of Fascists and became its Leader.

He was noted for his persuasive oratorial powers like his idol and mentor Adolf Hitler. Mosley and the BUF were responsible for stirring up anti-Semitic race riots in the years immediately prior to 1939.

On the outbreak of war he was arrested and detained under the Defence Regulations along with some of his adherents including several retired officers and a Member of Parliament.

Fig 57. BUF members at a Nuremberg rally.
Photo: Copress Munich

In 1936 Mrs Edward invited William Joyce to Sanquhar and arranged for him to address the masses in the Mechanics' Institute. Joyce was then Director of Propaganda for the British Union of Fascists.. Born in Brooklyn of an English mother and an Irish American father his family came to England in 1921. He fled to Germany just before the outbreak of war and gave weekly broadcasts from Radio Hamburg. His grating, sneering, arrogant voice earned him the title Lord Haw Haw, bestowed on him by the radio critic of the *Daily Express*. Neglecting to hand in his British passport before he left for Germany was to prove fatal for Joyce, as he was subsequently convicted of treason and hanged on 3rd January 1946.

In 1936 as Joyce harangued the audience of less than thirty in the Mechanic's Institute and fended off the interruptions from a drunken heckler, in distant Quetta in India, a senior officer at the Staff College was settling down to sleep. This was Bernard Law Montgomery, son of the Bishop of Tasmania, an army officer since 1908, mentioned in dispatches, and due eventually to progress to the highest rank in the British Army.

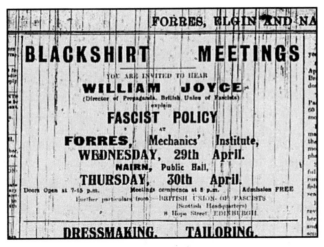

Fig 58. From: Forres, Elgin and Nairn
Gazette, Wednesday, April 29 1936.

When German troops marched into the Sudetenland, the scales fell off from the eyes of Mrs Edward and she renounced any connection or support for the Nazis and Fascists. When war came she and her husband gave up a large part of Sanquhar House as a convalescent home for wounded servicemen. In 1944 preparations for the invasion of Europe were well advanced. At suitable locations all over Britain, troops rehearsed again and again for these critical moments when they would transfer from the temporary relative security of their landing ship to the uncertainties of a mined and defended beach.

There were mistakes and accidents. Tanks prematurely slid off their ship transports and sudden squalls swept men and equipment overboard. Secrecy was paramount, not only must information be kept from any enemy agents, but the public must also be kept in the dark, less an unguarded word or comment could find its way to the enemy or, perhaps, cause alarm and despondency in the general population. One unverified incident involved the death by drowning of several soldiers who were laid out on the beach above high water mark. All the adjacent households were visited and the occupants were ordered to sign the Official Secrets Act and warned that if they ever mentioned the matter then they would go to jail.

Civilians and services alike were very conscious of the need for security, but, occasionally, security slipped into hysteria. On 5th February 1943 Colonel Blimp, aka Colonel Alex. Cattanach, Commander of the Moray Sub-Area, in Rotha House Elgin, wrote a blistering letter to Mr.G.R.MacKenzie, controller of the ARP in Forres, about some alleged breach of security. His first words were especially sinister "I have received through security a very disturbing report…." MacKenzie was able to refute the allegations, although he had to write a lengthy time-wasting letter explaining the circumstances. In reply he received a brief reply from the colonel's G.S.O.3 "I am to say that having read your explanation of the incident the Commander now considers this matter closed."

On the 27th March 1944, General Montgomery came to inspect and encourage the troops. His special train code named *Rapier*, complete with communication equipment, cooks and guards, puffed into Forres station and was shunted into a siding. According to his autobiography, 'By the middle of May I had visited every formation in the United Kingdom. I had been seen by practically every officer and soldier who was to take part in the invasion of Normandy, and they had heard me talking to them."

Clearly he could only see a fraction of those involved and it is not certain if he was even able to inspect all the men of the 3rd Division which he had commanded at Dunkirk and were now training in Moray.

What the great man did have time for was to go fishing on the Findhorn with his host, Alexander Edward. History is silent as to whether he caught anything and history is also silent as to whether he slept in the same bed as had once been occupied by Lord Haw-Haw.

Fig 59. Monty with Alexander Edward
on the banks of the Findhorn.
Photo: Courtesy of Robin MacKenzie

Conclusion

The Aftermath

This account has attempted to draw together a narrative of events that took place over sixty years ago in Moray and the neighbouring counties during the fateful years of the Second World War. The happenings of those days are now beginning to be of interest to a nation for most of whom it is history, as witness the frequent television programmes on the subject. It is also a period that is being researched by schools as part of the curriculum. The authors have been fortunate in being able to gather much valuable information from the few remaining survivors of the period and with wide ranging assistance from many people and organisations in the collection and assembly of the material.

The findings will be deposited in the record with Elgin Libraries, The Moray Society at Elgin Museum and with the Royal Commission on the Ancient and Historic Monuments of Scotland in Edinburgh for the information and interest of future generations.

However this is not simply about the gathering of artefacts and information. The interpretation of the importance and significance of the information for the people involved and their successors is equally important. In this Conclusion an attempt has been made to assess the effects that the events of the war years had on the economic, political and social lives of the people of Moray.

The announcement of the cessation of hostilities brought a sudden euphoria as the stress under which people had been living for so long was suddenly relieved. When the first excitement had died down however, people began to take stock, to see how the war years had changed their lives and to consider what the future might hold. The war dead from Morayshire totalled one woman and 517 men, whose names were added to the Roll of Honour for the dead of World War One.

Arising from the need to harness the national will and endeavours to the overriding aim of victory at all costs there had inevitably been many changes in popular culture, taste, style, fashion and public attitudes and opinion. Amongst the cultural, economic, social and political change in the fast moving society we had become there were lost in the process many of the old certainties and more especially the standards by which society acted. Many saw it as a lowering to the lowest common denominator, others saw it as a welcome release from the pre-war stuffiness that was the hangover from the dominance of Queen Victoria and good Prince Albert.

Economically Britain was virtually bankrupt, and industry, exhausted by a long sustained effort for victory, now had to buckle-to and earn its way to national solvency. On the social scene the freedom fifties gave way to the swinging sixties and the rise of flower power and the hems of skirts. On the political front we had Harold Wilson, Gannex Macs and Football Special trains at week-ends.

The wartime influx of troops into Moray had brought with it many new ideas and customs that found ready acceptance with the native residents and gave rise to many changes in our way of living. For example, before the war there was little fuss made to celebrate Christmas, perhaps a day off work for some and a small addition to the table for most; the main event was Hogmanay. Scots and English now celebrate Christmas with equal fervour and the English celebrate New Year with nearly the same enthusiasm as the Scots.

There were changes in the daily diet, too, that were largely due to restrictions as a result of rationing. The shortage of sugar, for example, produced a healthier diet. Other dishes concocted to recipes published by the ministry of food also contributed to a healthier diet. The famous 'Woolton Pie' comes to mind, (Appendix 8) named after Lord Woolton who was the responsible minister. Despite shortages, under the able guidance of Sir John Orr of the Rowett Institute in Aberdeen our national nutrition resulted in a healthier post-war Britain. The emancipation of women received a boost from the war largely as a result of the tremendous effort they made working for victory. The women's liberation movement continued the work.

As with practically every other facet of life the war was also responsible for changes in some areas of industry and commerce in Moray. There is no space here to examine the matter in detail; it is a subject that would justify a book on its own. In general the effect was to boost production to provide the 'sinews of war', but in some few cases the reallocation of materials to meet new demands meant reduction or even closure. The diversion of materials from the distilling industry to food production was a case in point. New industries were established such as the highly secret Hydrogen Gas Plant at Keith set up to supply gas for Barrage Balloons. Here the manpower released from the distilleries was virtually immediately absorbed by the new industry.

Many businesses received a boost from contracts to supply goods and services to the greatly expanded complement of military moved into the area. Elgin Motors, for example, was busy doing maintenance and repairs on military vehicles, and contractors were stretched to the limit with new construction works, particularly for the Army and the RAF.

But despite all the privations and initial military setbacks there was never any widespread feeling that we would lose the war. This was unthinkable. Even after Dunkirk, which was a massive defeat, but which was sold to the British as a victory, the feeling was that at last we were on our own and didn't need to worry about the dubious Belgians or the unreliable French. The time when morale sagged was the three months after Pearl Harbour and particularly when news came through that the two great battleships, the pride of the British Navy, the *Prince of Wales* and *Repulse* had been sunk by Japanese aircraft of 11th December 1941. This set-back was soon followed by the loss of Hong Kong and then Singapore. Some were buoyed up by a letter which had appeared in *John Bull* early in 1940. A lady wrote that she had experienced a most vivid dream where she saw thousands of people outside Buckingham Palace all cheering and waving and a big sign saying 'Victory-May 1945'. At the time 1945 seemed a very long time away but it was a comfort to remember that lady's dream in the dark days of 1941/42.

The Language

During the War the language of the day changed rapidly and some of the changes are still in use today. Words such as 'blitz', 'You'd better put a blitz on' and 'flak', 'Your suggestion ran into a lot of flak', are still in common usage though far removed from their original meaning of 'lightning' and 'anti-aircraft fire'. One word, much used in the services and now well established in colloquial English is 'chuffed'. This means 'well pleased' yet originally and in service parlance it meant the exact opposite and had the meaning of 'fed up'. Then there was 'dhobying' for laundry, a word carried over from the army's long sojourn in India. Being fed up to the back teeth was called being 'browned off'. 'Brothel creepers' were suede boots as worn in the desert campaign in preference to army issue black boots.

Just as careless talk could cost lives, so the unwise word or phrase could start hostilities between nominal allies. An innocent question from a Gordon to a Red Hackle (Black Watch) 'Faa shot the cheese?' was guaranteed to start a brawl between these, normally brotherly, regiments.(This explosive comment originated during the first world war when the Black Watch were in the line. At night the rations came up, including a large circular cheese, which was suspended on a stick carried by two men. The round cheese glowed in the moonlight and the men in the trench opened fire on this unknown monster which was approaching them. The Gordons never tire of reminding their Black Watch colleagues of this episode!)

French Canadians and British Canadians would fight at the drop of a hat or a phrase and it is believed that the epic battle of Forres, mentioned elsewhere, took place between these citizens of the one country. Inter-service rivalries were commonplace; the army particularly did not approve of the 'Brylcream boys', the airforce, while the Navy considered itself superior to the other junior services and referred to the army as 'brown jobs'. All were united in their detestation of the military police or 'Red Caps' who, behind their backs, they were occasionally known as kippers, 'two faced and no guts'. Recruits 'square bashed', 'drilled', and if unlucky, would be placed on 'jankers' or detention. If lucky there might be 'char', tea and a 'wad' or bun. A bed or bunk was referred to as a 'pit'. Uncomfortable enemy activity such as shelling or bombing was referred to as a 'hate' or a 'stonk'.

Aircraft never crashed, they 'pranged' and a 'wizard prang' was a spectacular crash. Tanks never caught fire, they 'brewed up', and the famous American Sherman tank used by all allied ground forces was so soft skinned that it nearly always 'brewed up' as soon as it was hit so the Germans called it a 'tommy cooker' for obvious reasons and the British called it a 'ronson lighter'. Anything familiar has many names and so it was with death. Nobody in the services died; maybe 'they went for a Burton' or 'bought it' or 'handed in their chips' or were 'written off'. U/s was an acronym for unserviceable and has survived into the language today. Anything good or pleasurable was always 'super'. In Europe any siesta was called 'blanket drill or 'studying one's profession'.

The army produced two wonderful purveyors of new words and expressions in the anti-establishment cartoon characters, the 'Two Types' were worthy successors to Bruce Bairnsfather's 'Old Bill', a First World War veteran of the trenches. These two officers, one a dark 'cavalry' type, the other a fair 'tank' type were the brainchild of Jon, or William John Philpin Jones, MBE, to give him his full name, and were born, or rather hatched, in the North African desert. There they 'swanned about', driving aimlessly and their post lunch siesta was taken up with 'Egyptian P.T.' or 'charping'.

'...and precisely what do you mean by improperly dressed?'

Anything they bought they paid for in 'akkers' all the while dreaming of 'Python'

Fig 60. A typical JON Cartoon
Courtesy of Mrs S.P. Jones

or leave; so called because it was so long drawn out. These two officers and all allied soldiers, fighting in the mud of Italy, (unkindly referred to as 'D-Day Dodgers' by Lady Astor in 1944 when the invasion of Europe began.- Jon.1991:183) were last seen being recalled to the colours for Suez in 1956, but since then, like the old soldiers they were, have simply faded away, leaving behind a half forgotten memory of words and acronyms.

A 'Jingle of Jargon' by R.M. recorded in 1946:

Said the airman to the skyman, "Now the global conflict dwindles,
Do a spot of gen-bestowing on an unenlightened erk-
Is it true the milkman humours non priority consumers,
Do you see the grocer planning an austerity Dunkirk?'

"There are hedgehogs," said the skyman "to be softened up and plastered-
There are pockets still to hit at, there are Anzios to crack;
Thunderbolts at tree top level have to prang them like the devil,
Peeling off to winkle round them, fanning out to push them back."

"Corridors are being driven through the armoured tips of bulges,
V-repairs proceed so slowly they're a topic for the wits;
But it stirs the public passion finding too much off-the-ration-
That means D Day", said the airman, "for a new blackmarket blitz."

"I'd an uncle", said the skyman, "with a hoard of Yankee candy;
When a doodle-bug approached him, he concluded that was that;
But has loss was only partial, as he told the shelter Marshall,
For his Morrison preserved it, though his Anderson was flat."

"We were spearheads in the v-war", said the airman to the skyman,
"And pounced on pick-a- back planes with a stern avenging whiz.
If a multi-level fly past doesn't make me think of my past,
Would utility peace-feelers make a neutral think of his?"

"What of Radar?" said the skyman "what of Mulberry and Python?
Even Crocodiles were hush-hush till the newsmen blew the gaff.
Does our proud successful side owe more to Pluto than to Fido,
SEAC, ENSA, NAAFI, AMGOT, UNRRA, REME or the RAF?"

"Came the peace switch, from VJ Day" said the airman to the skyman.
Many phrases lost their power to uplift or disconcert,
But I will say this: I'd rather be a pre-Pearl Harbour father
Than set out to smash a record in a new top secret squirt."

Although the famous JON cartoon figures were first seen in the *Eighth Army News* in August 1944, they were soon appearing as a regular feature in the weekly *Crusader* in November and in *The Soldier* from its first issue in March 1945 and so became equally firm favourites with the allied forces in Europe.

As General 'Sir Bernard Freyberg VC said:
'the two types were worth a Division of troops'

Fig 61. The 'Two Types' JON Cartoon
Courtesy of Mrs S.P. Jones

As Field-Marshall the Rt. Hon. Earl Alexander of Tunis says in a foreword to a recent book of JON's cartoons of the Two Types:

"a Britisher is naturally repugnant to any form of regimentation,
which of course includes what he has to wear…. he is a warrior and a
fighter but really a civilian and a man of peace at heart."

The dark one with his khaki-drill bush shirt and battered service-dress cap and the other fair one with his over stretched pullover and armoured regiment black beret and corduroy trousers, despite being caricatures, were fairly typical of the fighting troops, whether in the desert or elsewhere, that battles raged.

Fig 62. The futility of war
Photo: I K

A German lies beside a Briton in Lossiemouth cemetery.

We give the last word to W S Churchill, the Architect of Victory, who said on V E Day, 8th MAY 1945...

"In all our long history we have never seen a greater day than this. Everyone, men and women has done their best."

If reading this has awakened any memories that you would like to have included in a future edition the authors would be pleased to hear from you.

Bibliography

Anon 1945 - *The Story of 79th Armoured Division*.
Published privately.

Aanensen, A. 1974 - *Når vi kommer inn fra havet*.
Dreyers, Oclo.

The Air Ministry 1945 - *By Air to Battle*.
HMSO, London.

Barlow, J.A. 1942 - *Small Arms Manual*.
John Murray, London.

Bartlam, W.A. 2000 - *The Morayshire Brick and
Tile Works: A Vanished Industry*.
Moray Libraries, Elgin.

Bartlam, W.A. 2002 - *A History of the Fire Service
and its Establishment in Moray*.
Moray Libraries, Elgin.

Bartlam, W.A. 2002 - *Keith Gas Plant: A Brief History of
Keith Hydrogen Gas Plant and the World War Two
Barrage Balloons*.
Moray Libraries, Elgin.

Beauman, K.B. 1977 - *Greensleeves: The Story of WVS - WRVS*.
Seeley, London.

Bedoyère, G. de la. 2002 - *The Home Front*.
Shire Princes Risborough.

Bennett, R. (Ed.) 2001 - *Elgin Academy, 1801-2001:
A Celebration of 200 Years*.
Moravian Press Ltd., Elgin.

Boyd, Capt. A. Undated (c1944) - *A Brief History of The
1st Moray Battalion Home Guard. Affiliated to
The Seaforth Highlanders*.
Unpublished.

Brophy, J. and Partridge 1965 - *The Long Trail*.
Andre Deutsch, London.

Brown, A.C. 1988 - *The Secret Servant*.
Sphere Books Ltd., London.

Bryant, A. 1957 - *The Turn of the Tide: 1939-1943*.
Reprint Socy, London.

Buckley, C. 1941 - *Norway: The Commando's Dieppe*.
HMSO, London.

Buckton, H. 1993 - *Forewarned is Forearmed*.
Ashford, Buchan & Enright, Leatherhead.

Churchill, W.S.C. 1949 - *The Second World War*
Vol. II and Vol. IV.
Penguin 1985, London.

Cox, R. 1974 - *Operation Sealion*.
Arrow Books, London (Fiction).

Dear, I.C.B. (Ed.) 1995 - *The Oxford Companion
to the Second World War*.
Oxford University Press, Oxford.

Deighton, L. 1993 - *Blood Tears and Folly in the
darkest hour of the Second World War*.
Jonathan Cape, London.

Delaforce, P. 1995 - *Monty's Ironsides: From the Normandy
Beaches to Bremen with the 3rd division*.
Sutton, Stroud.

Delmer, S. 1962 - *Black Boomerang Vol 2*.
Secker & Warburg, London.

Dorman, J.E. 1996 - *Orkney Coast Batteries 1914 - 1956*.
Twin Six Productions, Kirkwall.

Ellis, J. 1993 - *World War II Data Book*.
BCA, London.

Farago, L. 1971 - *The Game of the Foxes*.
McKay, New York.

Fereday, R.P. (Ed.) 2000 - *Samuel Laing of Papdale 1780 - 1868*.
Bellavista Publications, Kirkwall.

Fleming, P. 1957 - *Invasion 1940*.
Hart Davis, London.

Fletcher, D. 1984 - *Vanguard of Victory:
The 79th Armoured Division*.
HMSO, London.

Forbes, A.H. 1975 - *Forres: A Royal Burgh 1150 - 1975*.
Moray and Nairn County Library, Elgin.

Gray, A. 1998 - *Timber*.
Tuckwell, East Linton.

Hastings, M. 1984 - *Overlord, D-Day and the Battle for Normandy*.
Michael Joseph, London.

Henderson, Dr D.M. 2002 - *The Scots at War Trust*.
Edinburgh.

Heyman, C. (Ed.) 1984 - *The British Army Pocket Guide*.
Pen & Sword Books Ltd., Barnsley.

Hinsley, F.H. and Simkins, C.A.G. 1979 / 90 -
British Intelligence in the Second World War Vol IV.
HMSO, London.

Howe, E. 1982 - *The Black Game*.
Michael Joseph, London.

Hughes, J. 1991 - *A Steep Turn to the Stars*.
Bevenagh Books, Peterborough.

Hutchinson's Encyclopaedia 2000.
Helicon Publishing, Oxford.

Innes, H. 1941 - *Attack Alarm*.
Collins, London (Fiction).

Jones, W.J.P. 1991 - *JON's Complete Two Types*.
Bellew Publishing Co. Ltd, London.

Jowitt, The Earl 1954 - *Some Were Spies*.
Hodder and Stoughton, London.

Kahn, D. 1978 - *Hitler's Spies*.
Hodder and Stoughton, London.

Keillar, I and Rose, A. 1984 - *Dad's Army:
The Home Guard in Moray 1940 - 44*.
Moray Field Club Bulletin 1985, Elgin Museum.

Keillar, I. 1990 - *The Sawdust Fusiliers*.
Unpublished.

Kochan, M. 1980 - *Prisoners of England*.
Macmillan, London.

Kochan, M. 1983 - *Britain's Internees in the Second World War.*
Macmillan, London.

Lampe, D. 1968 - *The Last Ditch*
Cassell, Secker & Warburk & Co., London.

Levy, Y. 1941 - *Guerilla Warfare.*
Penguin, London.

Longmate, N. 1991 - *Island Fortress: The Defence of
Great Britain 1603 - 1945.*
Hutchinson, London.

MacDonald, Dr J.C.M. 1990 - *Moray in the 1939 - 45 War.
Royal Navy, RNR and Merchant Navy. The 201st Auxiliary Unit.*
Moray Society Lecture, Elgin Museum.

Main, J. 2003 - *The First Nurse.*
Librario, Elgin.

Mallman Showell, J.P. 1989 - *U-Boat Command
and the Battle of the Atlantic.*
Conway Maritime Press, London.

Masterman, J.C. 1972 - *The Double Cross System.*
Yale University Press.

Maurice-Jones, Col. K.W. 1959 - *A History of
Coast Defence in the British Army.*
Royal Artillery Institution.

Melville, M.L. 1981 - *The Story of the Lovat Scouts 1900 - 1980.*
The St. Andrew Press, Edinburgh.

Messenger, C. 1995 - *The Century of Warfare:
Worldwide conflict from 1900 to the present day.*
Harper Collins, Glasgow.

Millar, E.A. 1991 (cited in Intro to) *Memories of 1940:
Impressions of life in an internment camp.*
By V. Rev. Mgr. Gaetano Rossi.
Associazione Culturale Scoglio di Frisio Foundation, Rome.

Moen, J. 1986 - *John Moe: Double Agent.*
Mainstream Publishing Co. Ltd., Edinburgh.

Montgomery, F.M., The Viscount B.L. of Alamein K.G. 1960 -
The Memoirs of Field-Marshal the Viscount Montgomery, K.G.
Fontana Books, London.

Newspapers:

Banffshire Herald
Elgin Courant and Courier
Forres Elgin and Nairn Gazette

Electronic References:

http://www.ads.ahds.uk/catalogue/search/resFormat.cfm
http://www.ads.ahds.ac.uk/catalogue/specColl/dob/ai_full_r.cfm?refno=15240
http://www.cometamagico.com.ar/maskelyne2.htm
http://www.pro.gov.uk/releases/nov2002_mi5/intro.htm
http://www.scotsatwar.org.uk/secret/spies.html
http://www.angelfire.com/dc/1spy/Lahousen.html
http://www.stahlbrandt.com/html/history/moewe.html

Issued by the Ministry of Information *in co-operation with the War Office and the Ministry of Home Security.*

If the

comes

WHAT TO DO — AND HOW TO DO IT

THE Germans threaten to invade Great Britain. If they do so they will be driven out by our Navy, our Army and our Air Force. Yet the ordinary men and women of the civilian population will also have their part to play. Hitler's invasions of Poland, Holland and Belgium were greatly helped by the fact that the civilian population was taken by surprise. They did not know what to do when the moment came. *You must not be taken by surprise.* This leaflet tells you what general line you should take. More detailed instructions will be given you when the danger comes nearer. Meanwhile, read these instructions carefully and be prepared to carry them out.

I

When Holland and Belgium were invaded, the civilian population fled from their homes. They crowded on the roads, in cars, in carts, on bicycles and on foot, and so helped the enemy by preventing their own armies from advancing against the invaders. You must not allow that to happen here. Your first rule, therefore, is :—

(1) IF THE GERMANS COME, BY PARACHUTE, AEROPLANE OR SHIP, YOU MUST REMAIN WHERE YOU ARE. THE ORDER IS " STAY PUT ".

If the Commander in Chief decides that the place where you live must be evacuated, he will tell you when and how to leave. Until you receive such orders you must remain where you are. If you run away, you will be exposed to far greater danger because you will be machine-gunned from the air as were civilians in Holland and Belgium, and you will also block the roads by which our own armies will advance to turn the Germans out.

II

There is another method which the Germans adopt in their invasion. They make use of the civilian population in order to create confusion and panic. They spread false rumours and issue false instructions. In order to prevent this, you should obey the second rule, which is as follows :—

(2) DO NOT BELIEVE RUMOURS AND DO NOT SPREAD THEM. WHEN YOU RECEIVE AN ORDER, MAKE QUITE SURE THAT IT IS A TRUE ORDER AND NOT A FAKED ORDER. MOST OF YOU KNOW YOUR POLICEMEN AND YOUR A.R.P. WARDENS BY SIGHT, YOU CAN TRUST THEM. IF YOU KEEP YOUR HEADS, YOU CAN ALSO TELL WHETHER A MILITARY OFFICER IS REALLY BRITISH OR ONLY PRETENDING TO BE SO. IF IN DOUBT ASK THE POLICE-MAN OR THE A.R.P. WARDEN. USE YOUR COMMON SENSE.

Map of BLACK FRIDAY

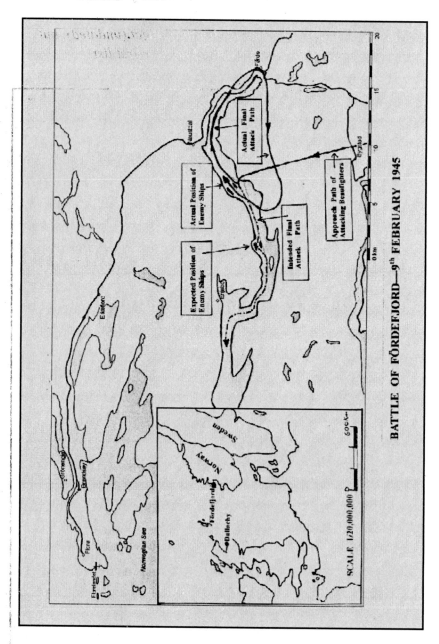

Nominal Roll of
Moray Home Guard Auxiliary Units.

Information from Defence of Britain project (undated), but assumed to be an early, if not the first list.

MOST SECRET

AUXILIARY UNITS No.2 AREA NOMINAL ROLL

Spey Bay Patrol

Lt   L. Cochrane
Sgt J. McLean
Cpl J. Robertson
Pte J. Grant
Pte A. Gordon
Pte A. Hepburn
Pte W. Hepburn
Pte F. McLean
Pte J. McLean
Pte T.F. Tocher
Pte C. Young

Clochan/Buckie

Sgt S. Grigor
Cpl J. Allan
Pte W. Farquarson
Pte A. McPherson
Pte G. Kelann
Pte C. Taylor

Keith/Grange Patrol

2Lt G. Fisher
Sgt W. Ingram
Cpl A. Pirie
Pte J. Munro
Pte D. Cruickshank
Pte J. Henderson
Pte J. Irvine
Pte J. Reid
Pte J. Robertson

Deskford Patrol

Sgt W. Smith
Cpl W. Currie
Pte I. Bowie
Pte G. Currie
Pte S. Milne
Pte W. Pirie
Pte T. Rumbles
Pte P. Smith

Darnaway Patrol

Sgt R. Reid
Cpl G. Reid
Pte D. MacIntyre
Pte D. MacLennan
Pte G. MacLennan
Pte J. Stephen

Forres/Kinloss

Sgt C. Murray
Cpl W. Laing
Pte G. Burgess
Pte J. MacIntosh
Pte G. McAulay
Pte W. Russell
Pte H. Collie

Alves/Spynie/Elgin Patrol

2Lt D. Denoon
Sgt J. Brown
Cpl J. Ogg
Pte A. Allen
Pte J. Mustard
Pte A. Sinclair
Pte W. Munro
Pte A. Mutch
Pte L. McWilliam
Pte R. Proctor
Pte A. Wiseman

Lhanbryde/Orton/Fochabers Patrol

Sgt N. Hepburn
Cpl J. Ritchie
Pte J. Geddes
Pte K.S. MacGregor
Pte H. Hampton
Pte J.P. Milne
Pte J. Riddell

The Blacker Bombard 29-MM SPIGOT MORTAR

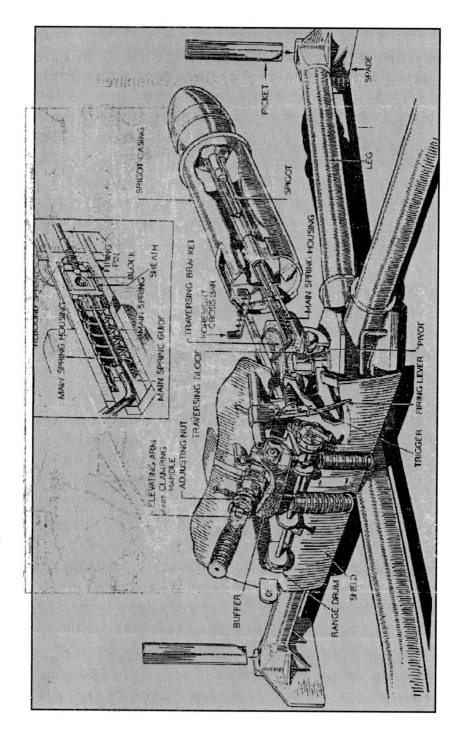

Training and target beaches compared

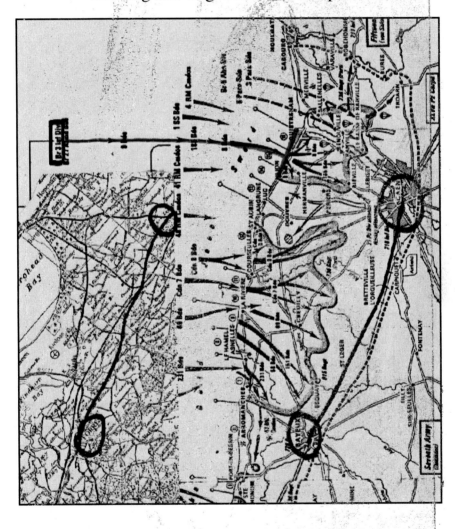

LORD WOOLTON PIE

The ingredients for this pie can be varied according to the vegetables in season.

Potato, swede, cauliflower and carrot make a good mixture.

Take 1 lb of them, diced, 3 or 4 spring onions, if possible, 1 teaspoonful vegetable extract and 1 table-spoonful of oatmeal.

Cook together for 10 minutes with just enough water to cover. Stir occasionally to prevent the mixture from sticking.

Allow to cool, put into a pie-dish, sprinkle with chopped parsley and cover with a crust of potato or wheatmeal pastry.

Bake in a moderate oven until the pastry is nicely browned and serve hot with a brown gravy. Enough for 4 or 5.

If you are short of fat, use this pie-crust which is made without fat:

Mix together 8 ozs, wheatmeal flour,
            1 level teaspoonful baking powder,
            a pinch of salt,
            a pinch of powdered sage if liked.
Stir in nearly   pint of cold milk, or milk and water.
Roll out the mixture and use it as you would an ordinary crust, but serve the pie *hot*.

Agents in training.

The photograph, allegedly taken by an instructor, shows Vera Eriksen and her two accomplices practising in a rubber dinghy from a Heinkel HE 115 off the Norwegian coast. The seaplane used in the operation, (p.128) on 30th September 1940, is variously described as a Heinkel HE 115 or a Bloem and Voss flying boat.

(Unternehmen Moewe
http://www.stahlbrandt.com/html.history/moewe.hyml.)

ABOUT THE AUTHORS

Bill Bartlam was 22 when he quit university to join the Army at the start of the war in 1939. By Christmas he was in France with the BEF, until he escaped at Dunkirk. On return to the UK he applied for transfer to the Royal Engineers and was posted to Pinefield Camp Elgin for re-training. Commissioned in May 1942 he was posted to 5 Assault Regiment RE, which fought its way from the beaches on 'D' Day into Germany with 3 British Division.

He was demobilised in May 1946 and returned to his studies and after qualifying as an Architect he set up his own practice in Elgin in 1947. 35 years later he retired and re-qualified as an Archaeologist since when he has written many monographs about Elgin's Industries, past and present. This project is undertaken in collaboration with Ian Keillar with whom he shares an interest in the Romans in Scotland.

Ian Keillar was born in Kinross in 1924 and volunteered for the Royal Air Force in 1942. After training at Arbroath and Bolton he served for eighteen months as a signals specialist with Bomber Command. Sent to the Middle East he spent V-E Day (8th May 1945) in Egypt and for the next two and a quarter years travelled all over the Middle East, from Baghdad to Benghazi and Cyprus to Sharjah, eventually being demobilised, with the rank of corporal, in August 1947.

Subsequently, as a Chartered Electrical Engineer, he came to Elgin in 1964 and worked with the North of Scotland Hydro-Electric Board. Married with three children and seven grandchildren he lives in Bishopmill, Elgin and has written on archaeology and history.

205